POPE FRANCIS TAKES THE BUS

and other unexpected stories

ROSARIO CARELLO

servant
AN IMPRINT OF
FRANCISCAN MEDIA
Cincinnati, Ohio

Scripture passages have been taken from *New Revised Standard Version Bible, copyright* ©1989 by the Division of Christian Education of the National Council of the Churches of Christ in the USA, and used by permission. All rights reserved.

First published in Italian as *I Racconti de Papa Francesco* in 2013 by Edizioni San Paolo. First UK edition, *Little Flowers of Pope Francis,* was published in 2014 by St. Pauls Publishing. Translated by George Woodall.

Cover and book design by Mark Sullivan
Cover illustration © Roberto Rinaldi

LIBRARY OF CONGRESS CATALOGING-IN-PUBLICATION DATA
Names: Carello, Rosario, author.
Title: Pope Francis takes the bus, and other unexpected stories / Rosario Carello.
Other titles: Racconti di Papa Francesco. English
Description: Cincinnati : Servant, 2016. | Previously published under title: Little flowers of Pope Francis : UK : St. Pauls Publishing, 2014. |
Includes bibliographical references.
Identifiers: LCCN 2016010642 | ISBN 9781632531308 (alk. paper)
Subjects: LCSH: Francis, Pope, 1936- | Popes—Biography—Anecdotes.
Classification: LCC BX1378.7 .C38513 2016 | DDC 282.092—dc23
LC record available at http://lccn.loc.gov/2016010642
ISBN 978-1-63253-130-8

Published by Servant
an imprint of Franciscan Media
28 W. Liberty St.
Cincinnati, OH 45202
www.FranciscanMedia.org

Printed in the United States of America.
Printed on acid-free paper.
17 18 19 20 5 4 3

Contents

Pope Francis has surprised us, time and again. In just the first year of his pontificate he has simply adopted a new way of being pope and Bishop of Rome. The examples are numerous. They began in the very first few days of his election with his less formal style of dress, his choice to live at the Casa Santa Marta, his use of a small car in place of a limousine, his frequent personal phone calls to friends and complete strangers. The list goes on. He has done all this without a word of criticism of his predecessors, Pope Emeritus Benedict XVI and Pope St. John Paul II. In fact, far from criticizing them, he has made frequent and very eloquent tributes to their holiness, their own apostolates and achievements. He continues to emphasize and draw from their teaching.

So much has already changed, and the changes go on. There were some who claimed that the initial changes were superficial and would only make a minimal impact in the short term. In fact, there are clearly many substantial projects that cannot be rushed but whose progress is evident. Their completion and their impact will stretch well into the future. The most obvious long-term undertaking is the work of the eight cardinals on the review of the Roman Curia and the assessment of the role of the Vatican Bank. Such large institutions take time to be studied and analyzed. It will also take a considerable amount of time to see what impact the pope's very frequently voiced concerns for the poor and the suffering can have on the way the Church, not only in the Vatican but throughout the world, learns to respond in new and practical ways to all forms of poverty and destitution.

Whether intended or not, the making of these changes and the whole style of this papacy has drawn the interest of millions of people both within the Church and far beyond its membership. Being named "Person of the Year" by *Time* magazine was an indication of Pope Francis's global impact. What was rather more surprising was his being named "Person of the Year," a week later, by *The Advocate* magazine, an American magazine that promotes gay rights. This suggests that Francis has broken into new territory where he might have previously been expected to be ignored or dismissed as speaking for a Church of unchanging moral attitudes.

We can see in Pope Francis a radical change in priorities that are being declared in his words but also evidenced by his actions and personal way of life. In the pages that follow there is much to be learned about Pope Francis. They present a portrait of someone who as a single individual, without doubt, is touching the lives of millions of people. In his daily life he is showing us how he understands the Gospel message and his response to that understanding. Let us see how much we may learn about him and then consider what that new knowledge and understanding might mean for us.

The Most Reverend John Arnold
Bishop of the Diocese of Salford
Province of Liverpool, England

NOTE ON THE TEXT

Just as Jules Verne imagined traveling around the world in eighty days, so I have tried to tell the story of Pope Francis in eighty stories.

Pope Francis was elected in 2013. This book contains stories and episodes from various stages in his life: parish priest, rector, bishop, archbishop, cardinal, pope. Throughout his career he has liked to be known as Padre (Father) Bergoglio. For this reason, without losing sight of the various offices of the Church he has served throughout his ministry, in the text he is often also referred to as Fr. Bergoglio.

1.

A IS FOR...ATTENTIVENESS

Fr. Bergoglio is expected at the other side of Buenos Aires for a day of recollection. He is in a hurry. He still has to catch the train.

He leaves his office, passes along the corridor, and enters the chapel. He pauses before the Blessed Sacrament. He prays in silence, entrusting to the Lord the talk he is going to give. He then immediately rushes out toward the exit. If he hurries, maybe he'll catch the train and be on time.

But before he can pass through the door, he hears his name being called. It is a young man. He looks unstable. Perhaps he is under the influence of mind-altering drugs. The young man asks Fr. Bergoglio to hear his confession.

"There is a priest about to come. Go to confession to him because I have some other things to do," Fr. Bergoglio replies.

Later, he was sorry for not being more attentive to the young man. In his interview with Francesca Ambrogetti, Pope Francis reflects regretfully on what he said to the young man: "I, a witness to the Gospel, spoke in this way." He explains that in that moment, as he was about to go out, four thoughts passed through his mind in a matter of seconds.

First: "I must hurry, they are waiting for me."
Second: "The other priest will not arrive all that quickly."
Third: "The boy is under the influence of drugs; he will not even realize how long he was waiting."
Fourth: "But what am I doing?"

Once outside, under the hot Argentine afternoon sun, Bergoglio stops himself. He raises his eyes to heaven, lowers them again, and turns back and walks slowly toward the young man. He says, "The father [priest] will be late. I will hear your confession."

It will be a confession that will take all the time that is necessary. Then the future pope calmly accompanies the young man to the statue of Our Lady where he entrusts him to her care. Afterward, only after this, he will go to the station in the certainty that he has missed the train.

He will have to wait for another one.

But God is the Lord of all. To his great surprise, Fr. Bergoglio discovers that the train is late and that he does not have to wait for another one. That evening, on his way home, he decides to stop off at his confessor's. He absolutely needs to ask forgiveness from God for what he has done, otherwise, he says, "Tomorrow I will not even be able to celebrate Mass."

But what is he to confess? The business with the young man? Bergoglio has questioned his own behavior, has understood his error, and corrected it. Francesca Ambrogetti explains to me: "Look, those few minutes or perhaps seconds in which he left that young man alone needed to be placed into the hands of God. The sense of shame he experienced for those few moments, the sense of sin he felt, were truly strong."

This is a crucial episode in the life of the Argentine pope. It enabled him to understand that it is not efficiency but patience that is the virtue of a person of faith. It does not matter how many things you do; it is the love you bring to them that makes the difference.

This is a lesson valid for the whole of his life. It is a lesson that Pope Francis learned not as a boy, nor in the seminary. He wasn't even starting out in his ministry. At the time he was already a bishop. The need to try to hear the voice of God, to listen to him at every moment of the day, was what the future pope learned from that experience.

2.

B IS FOR...BAPTISMS

There once was a widow, a very humble woman who was the mother of seven children from two different men. She was on her own and made her living as a cleaner. She had given up her dreams a long time ago. The last fragment of a wish that remained with her was to see her children baptized.

But what can she do? There are seven of them. Where will she find seven sets of godparents? And what will it cost, between feasts and invited guests? And then there is her work. How can she lose all that time, when she works every waking moment to provide what her family needs?

The woman has learned never to stop, to accept all the requests she receives. But year after year the children become bigger and her dream becomes smaller. One day she meets Archbishop Bergoglio. "Father, I am in mortal sin. I have seven children and I have never had them baptized," she says.

The future pope smiles at her. "Don't worry," he says.

They make an appointment, and a few days later the woman is in the curia. As soon as he hears what the situation is, Bergoglio removes the obstacles (or false obstacles).

"Let's do all the baptisms with [the same] two godparents; it's easier. And for the refreshments, there'll be cola and sandwiches after the ceremony."

The great day arrives. It is a catechesis that Bergoglio himself defines as "small." All of the children are baptized. What an unforgettable day for that mother!

"Father, I can't believe it. You make me feel important," says the widow.

Bergoglio replies, "But, what have I got to do with it? It is Jesus who makes you important."

For Bergoglio, baptizing children is a major priority, a necessity. "We must do everything we can to make baptisms possible," he tells the priests, some of whom had a rigid mentality and thought it was not a good thing to baptize the children of couples not married in church. "Is it the children's fault, if their parents are not married in church?" the future pope used to ask with a raised voice. Certainly not!

He knew well that more than a few couples, after the baptism and after making friends with the parish priest and coming to know the catechists, have asked to be married in church. He understood that there is no pastoral work if we don't establish genuine relationships with people. And we should never underestimate the power of God. In the sacrament of baptism, with the baptism of the children of a parent or parents, God enters joyfully into the daily experience of an entire family.

3.

B IS FOR...BENEDICT XVI

The first person to know of the election of Francis was Benedict XVI. The first telephone call that the new pope made was to the Pope Emeritus. Likewise, the first prayer that Francis requested as he stood on the balcony of St. Peter's was for Benedict.

At their meeting at Castel Gandolfo on March 23, 2013, the two men embraced. I was struck by the fact that, when addressing his predecessor, Bergoglio used the respectful *Lei* when addressing Ratzinger in Italian (rather than the familiar *tu* used between close friends and family).

There is harmony and continuity between the two men. If you want an example, read this: "Careerism, the attempt to climb upwards, to obtain a position by way of the Church, to be served, not to serve: this is the image of a man who, by way of the priesthood, wants to make himself important, to become a person of note; this is the image of someone who has his sights set on his own exaltation and not on the humble service of Jesus Christ."

Who said these strong words that cut like a sword? Are they the words of Pope Francis, who has often spoken about careerism in the Church and about worldly spirituality? No. The words quoted above are those of Benedict XVI. Ratzinger opened up the way for Bergoglio in all senses, not just by his resignation, but also by his pontificate. Resigning was both courageous and full of drama. Benedict XVI was subjected to harsh criticism for it. He often found himself alone. The Pope Emeritus displayed great personal courage.

4.

B IS FOR...BIRTHDAY

Pope Francis was born on December 17, 1936. But if you are thinking of giving him a present, you should know that he does not want to be the focus of the celebration. To be sure he is a joyful man, but he prefers going to celebrations that honor others.

5.

B IS FOR...BOOKS

Jorge Bergoglio prefers classic literary works such as those by Manzoni, Dostoevsky, Dante, and Borges. In the school year 1964–1965 the future Fr. Bergoglio taught literature at the Immaculate Conception College at Santa Fe. The students of the time recall this young man very well. Not yet a priest, he was passionate about literature. His superiors had asked him to become a teacher of a subject from among the humanities, even though he had studied the sciences.

The students also recall vividly the day on which Bergoglio announced to the class, more surprised than proud, that Jorge Luis Borges had accepted an invitation to come to meet them. This great writer stayed with the students for five days. They were some of the most fortunate students in history: There before them at one and the same time was one of the greatest writers of the twentieth century...and the future pope.

6.

B IS FOR...BUS

It is evening. Fr. Bergoglio has just finished celebrating Mass in a parish, and the concluding procession has come to an end. People are gathered in the sacristy, to put the sacred vestments back in place. "Excuse me," says Bergoglio to the people all around him who are winding down, the day's tasks completed. "Excuse me, but I have to go to Mataderos. Does anyone know which bus I need to take?"

All of a sudden, they all fall silent. Should they simply answer his question, or overcome the problem by offering the archbishop a ride? "There is no need for the bus," says one enterprising parishioner, stepping forward. "I will give you a lift in my car."

"No, thank you," says Archbishop Bergoglio. "I'm only asking you to tell me which bus I need to take from here."

"Allow me," says another parishioner. "I will take you. Mataderos is on the other side of the city and it is awkward by bus."

"No." Bergoglio shakes his head with emphasis. "Thank you. Just tell me which bus it is."

A third and a fourth gentleman, almost in chorus, say: "We insist, Father. We will take you. We can't let you go on your own."

This time the response is commanding: "I said no, my sons. I am going by bus."

"Very good," they all respond, a little embarrassed.

A little later, with fond words of thanks and farewell, Bergoglio makes his way on his own toward the bus stop, and on to another of the day's appointments. One young girl comments: "He certainly never stops."

And the parish priest says: "He goes as he came, on public transport."

The deacon adds: "Fr. Bergoglio is like that; he speaks by giving example."

The bus comes. Bergoglio gets on. At Mataderos they are waiting for him.

7.

C IS FOR…CHILDREN'S FEAST

Manuel slides out of bed, no need to be woken up.
"Manuel, I bet it's today, isn't it?"

"What's today?"

"Bergoglio's feast day."

"How do you know that, mum?"

Teresita knows her nine-year-old son only too well. She
knows that there is only one day in the year when she
does not have to blast him awake with a shout. That day
is the day of the Children's Feast, Fr. Bergoglio's pastoral
masterpiece for children. It was a feast for children who
had no knowledge of feasts or presents or sweet drinks
and the like because these children lived on the mud roads
and slept in huts.

Fr. Bergoglio always handled the event himself, and it
used to light up the suburb. It was a very poor suburb
around the Maximo College and St. Joseph Parish, in

the diocese of St. Michael (Colegio Máximo de San José, San Miguel). The whole parish was invaded. At least five thousand children always turned up. It was a feast for them—prepared just for them. And if you have any experience of children and of parishes, you will agree that five thousand is not an easy number of children to manage.

What was it like?

There was the theater with adventure stories of the great figures of the faith. The best-loved story was about the Jesuit missionaries on their way through the forest. The story of St. Ignatius also went down splendidly. There were also popular games and football. There were moments of prayer, catechetical groups, and naturally lunch. But the key moment that every child eagerly anticipated was the time for receiving presents. The moments before they were able to hold their present in their own hands gave them a thrilling, almost uncontainable joy that ran right through the children from their heads right down to their feet. Suddenly, rolled into one celebration, were their Christmas, their Epiphany, their birthday, their saint's day, and their Santa Lucia. Indeed for many of the children the Children's Feast was the only gift-giving occasion in the whole year. Without Bergoglio, there wouldn't have been even that.

But where do you find five thousand free presents? The Jesuit Bergoglio's imagination was without limits. He just asked for them as he went around the shops of the city. At the time he was not even a bishop. He turned to families with grown-up children to ask them to give away things they no longer used, toys and the like that could be presents. Sometimes the donated things were broken. So he set up a group of lads in the college—future Jesuits—in factories, specializing in doing repairs. It was organized to a very high standard.

8.

C IS FOR...CONFIDING IN PARENTS

To whom did Jorge Mario Bergoglio speak most easily as a boy? In whom did he confide? His mother, Regina? His father, Mario? In Rosa, his paternal grandmother, who played a crucial role in his upbringing? Apart from his grandmother, whom we'll meet later, it is undoubtedly his father who was the person he found it easiest to speak to.

In 1957 it was to his father that, at the age of twenty-one, the younger Bergoglio confides his greatest secret: "Dad, I have decided. I want to become a priest." He reveals this four years after the event at confession, which threw open his heart to the will of God, an episode that was illuminating and supernatural in some respects (see "V is for...Vocation," p. 140).

But what does it mean to say he had the most confidence in his father? It means he was sure that he would be listened to in times of difficulty, even sorrow, such as when he left home to enter into seminary. It means he had the certainty that he would find support from his father and not obstacles.

The young man was not wrong to have confidence in his dad. Mario listens attentively to the decision of his son. He is pleased but asks him if he is sure. Mario will speak of this decision to his wife, Jorge's mother. As you may have now guessed and as the youthful Jorge Bergoglio probably foresaw, his mother Regina does not take it well.

Regina Sivori is a woman of great faith. But she is not convinced about her son's choice. On one hand, her son is too young. On the other hand, she sees him as too grown-up already—he has a job and she sees him going in another direction. The fact remains that she does not accompany him to the seminary. However, she is there in the front row on the day of his ordination. There she will also kneel before him to receive his first blessing.

The kindest words, though, are from his grandmother, Rosa, his paternal grandmother: "If God is calling you, then may he bless you. But don't forget that the door of this house is always open and no one will ever criticize you if you decide to turn back."

9.

C IS FOR...COOKING

Sunday at the Maximo College is a day of rest. For everyone. And that includes the cook. In keeping with her contract, she stays at home.

So, who cooks for the students? No problem. Fr. Bergoglio is on hand. It's not only because it's in his nature to be at the service of others; it's also because he knows how to cook and to cook well. His mother taught him how to cook. The occasion when this began was not one of the happiest—at times we find a treasure even in the midst of the most difficult situations.

After being paralyzed (from which she recovered over time), his mother, Regina, experienced some difficulty in moving. So for long periods she had to stay seated and give instructions to her children, especially for lunch and for supper: "Take the flour," "Lower the heat," "Toss the pasta."

I have met many of the boys from that time, who used to eat at the Maximo on Sundays. I asked them: "What was Bergoglio's cooking like?"

"We ate almost better with him than on the weekdays," they replied.

But the future pope, in an interview with Francesca Ambrogetti, evaded the question with a joke: "I never killed anyone."

10.

C IS FOR...COURAGE

The telephone rings, just once. Fr. Bergoglio responds immediately and the conversation is brief. Without another word, the future pope picks up his jacket and leaves.

He walks for hours, asks for help, and goes where he thinks he will obtain it. He prays in silence, accepts that the times are not promising for Argentina. It is October 1976, seven months after the coup d'état. Soldiers have kidnapped John. That is the news burning inside Bergoglio's head.

Who is John? The young Italo-Argentine layman studied theology at the Jesuit Maximo College at San Miguel (Colegio Máximo de San Miguel) and has known Bergoglio for many years. His heart is alive with the words of the future pope. Along with some others, John has decided to move from words to actions: "Fr. Jorge, I want to go to live in the tent cities or shantytowns."

Fr. Bergoglio is proud of these youngsters. However, they weren't born in the shantytowns of the Villas Miserias of Buenos Aires, where they now spend most of their time. They have come to the attention of the military. This is the context of his concern for John.

Do the soldiers stop to check the facts, or to ask the women who have been guests at the help centers, such as Estella or Camilla, about the work these young men are doing? No, the soldiers do not ask such questions. Instead they watch suspiciously, and do not try to understand.

Bergoglio's worry is precisely this: that they just will not understand. For them the help centers are just a front. To the soldiers they are a cover where rebellion is fostered and organized. There, in the Villas, two worlds collide. On one side is to be found the gratuitous self-giving of John and of Bergoglio's boys. On the other, under the cruel presidential dictatorship of Jorge Videla, there is the military's culture of suspicion.

Initially the military had burst into John's house and tore it apart, seeking arms, which they did not find. Then, in October 1976, they kidnapped him.

For eighteen days, while Fr. Bergoglio searches all over for John, the young man is beaten, tortured, starved. In the end John is left to die in the middle of a street. But instead of being finished off in a hidden location, he is actually still alive because of that priest, Bergoglio, who has been knocking on every door.

In the years of the dictatorship, Bergoglio hid numerous people fleeing from the military in the Maximo College. He succeeded in freeing a significant number of kidnapped people. He met Videla on two occasions to discover the whereabouts of kidnapped priests. This is the most hidden side of Bergoglio, not because it is obscure, but because less has been said about it and also because of the humility of the key person involved. For Francis, it does not do to be considered a hero. There exist too many people to be listed who are alive and who were saved by the courage of the Jesuit future pope.

11.

C IS FOR...CREDO

A few days before being ordained priest by Archbishop Ramon José Castellano on December 13, 1969, Jorge Bergoglio wrote the following prayer and called it "Credo." I present it here as it was presented by the papers in the days after his election:

I want to believe in God the Father, who loves me as a son, and in Jesus the Lord, who has infused his spirit into my life to make me smile and so to bring me to the kingdom of eternal life.

I believe in my history, which has been spent under the gaze of the love of God and who, on the day when spring begins, 21 September, came to meet me to invite me to follow him.

I believe in my sorrow, without fruit because of the selfishness in which I take refuge.

I believe in the meanness of my soul, which always wants to take without ever giving.

I believe that other people are good and that I must love them without having any fear and without ever betraying them to provide myself with greater security.

I believe in the religious life.

I believe that I want to love much.

I believe in the death of every day, burning into me, from which I flee, but which laughs at me, inviting me to accept it.

I believe in God, patient, welcoming, good like a summer's night.

I believe that Dad is in heaven with God.

I believe that Fr. Duarte, also, is there, interceding for my priesthood.

I believe in Mary, my mother, who loves me and who will never leave me on my own.

And I look forward every day to the surprising ways in which love, strength, betrayal, and sin will be revealed, until that definitive meeting with that wonderful face, that face, although I do not know what it looks like, from which I flee continually, but which I want to know and to love. Amen.

12.

C IS FOR...CRIB

God lives in the city. This is Bergoglio's strong conviction because in urban settings people are called to live together, overcoming violence, poverty, and individualism. They need to meet Jesus, walking along those streets, so their lives might be transformed like so many of those who encountered him while he walked the earth. Think of Zacchaeus, Bartimaeus, and the woman with the hemorrhage.

Perhaps it was for this reason that, during a year in which the city changed its face notably, Cardinal Bergoglio promoted an initiative of historic importance to Buenos Aires. It was an initiative both ancient and spectacular and a delight for grown-ups and children alike. But let us not get ahead of ourselves.

At Christmas all cities become more beautiful. The paradox is that they become more beautiful because of Christmas, but people often forget the reason why there is a Christmas. Hence there was a need for an idea that would get people thinking and at the same time spark their emotions, opening up their hearts to wonder, as the crib (or manger) of Bethlehem still succeeds in doing. For this reason, in the pope's city, there are cribs on motortrucks full of lights and color and music as they travel around. In this way the mystery of Christmas is brought to all parts of the city. It is a beautiful Christmas procession. It is a call and recall to faith. It is a Church of the streets, a sharing with the people.

D IS FOR...DAD

Jorge was born in Argentina. He came to know Italy only through the words of his grandparents, who had left Italy deliberately to follow a plan of bringing the family back together again. So it was that the pope's dad, Mario, arrived in Buenos Aires at the difficult age of twenty-one. He met Regina there in 1934, and he married her one year later. Although it was in Buenos Aires that Mario intended to build his life and his whole world, nevertheless he had Italy in his heart and the separation had a dramatic effect.

Bergoglio tells us that his father reacted in a strange way when he spoke about their home in Piedmont, about the language, about his memories of Italy. It must have cost him a great deal to leave home, and this nostalgia remained with him strongly throughout his life. This is the fate of many emigrants. But Mario also proves himself to be a man capable of beginning again when things begin to go wrong. It is he who presses Jorge to work at the end of his third year in middle school. It is probably also he who decides on higher studies for his son. Mario is also the first person Jorge confides in when he wants to tell someone about discovering his vocation

From his dad, Jorge has learned to love silence and to have respect for suffering. Mario has taught his son self-denial, the meaning of the family, and the ethic of work.

14.

D IS FOR...DEATH

Bergoglio was on the point of dying when he was twenty-one years old.

He had seen his parents die, as well as three of his four siblings. Suffering has entered into his life and into his family. From such moments of sadness he has drawn a personal lesson, as he recounted to Rabbi Skorka: "I have seen die those who came before me. Now it is my turn. I don't know when."

Bergoglio defines death as "a companion in our daily life," about which he thinks constantly, to give value to every day and to add perspective and absolute meaning to the time he has to live, reminding him that time is a gift. Does death cause him to be afraid? Yes, and that is normal because it is a separation; "but, when we are on the point of taking flight, God places his hand upon us," because "he is the God of life, not the God of death. Death entered into the world with the devil."

15.

D is for...Devil

If you ask Pope Francis if he believes in the existence of the devil, the answer will be yes. Indeed, he will add, the greatest victory of the devil in our times has been brought about precisely by getting people to believe that he does not exist.

Yes, the devil exists and he is the father of all that is bad: calumny, hatred, division, and destruction. Francis has said on many occasions that all these come from Satan, the "father of lies" as he is called in the Bible.

As St. Ignatius used to teach and as Bergoglio knows very well, in each of us there exist three types of thought. One comes from our nature—that is to say, from our liberty and our will. The other two types of thought come from the outside: the good thoughts, which come from God, and the bad thoughts, which are from the devil. Thus, before our eyes we may say, a boxing ring is constructed in which good and evil, good thoughts and bad thoughts, confront each other. The decisive punches, those that hurt and lay us low and that determine who wins the round, we ourselves throw through our own choices.

Jorge Bergoglio very much likes St. Paul's image, according to which the Christian life is like a race, an athletic activity, in which we are to train ourselves, stripping away that which distances us from God.

"Evil exists," the pope said on June 12, 2013, in St. Peter's Square, "and the devil is active. But I would like to say at the top of my voice: God is stronger. Do you believe this, that God is stronger?"

A few seconds later, a clamorous "yes" resounded through the square.

16.

D IS FOR...DEVOTION (A PERSON OF)

When he was rector of the Maximo College, Fr. Bergoglio thought up and personally edited a little book. It was published at least thirty years ago. In Spanish, the book is called *Devocionario*, but in Italian it had to be called "Book of Prayers," because the term *devocionario*, although clear in Italian, does not exist in the Italian dictionary. (In English *devocionario* might also be translated as "person of devotion.")

The future pope's idea was simple: to give to all the boys, future Jesuit priests, a collection of major prayers and devotions. But which ones should be included?

The first, the most important for Bergoglio, is to the Sacred Heart, of which he says, "It is not an imaginary symbol. It is a real symbol, which represents the center, the fountain, from which the salvation of the entire human race has poured out."

None of the prayers loved by Catholics is missing: the rosary, the Angelus, Eucharistic Adoration, the renewal of baptismal promises, the Stations of the Cross, the novenas, and other devotions to the saints, among whom St. Joseph and St. Cajetan (patron of food and of work) and St. Thérèse of Lisieux stand out.

I have held a copy of this little, dark-colored book in my hands. The book, edited to the finest detail, can be put in your pocket. It's light and divided logically. The paper may not be of high quality, but it is robust. The illustrations are in black and white. It is the fruit of a work that stems from the desire to transmit treasure of the greatest value, treasure that Francis himself had received and that he wished to pass on to the boys of his college: prayer—personal, intimate, and continual.

17.

D IS FOR...DO NOT BE AFRAID

When [after the resurrection] Jesus appears in the Upper Room in the midst of the disciples, the doors were closed. The crucifixion—the ultimate punishment for a criminal in Roman times—and its aftermath had frightened them. Yet Jesus says to them, "Do not be afraid."

When the angel awakens the shepherds on Christmas night, he says, "Do not be afraid."

And when the archangel Gabriel meets Mary, in the mystery of the annunciation, he reassures her, "Do not be afraid."

These four marvelous words, "Do not be afraid," are the same words that John Paul II brandished like a stick against the enemies of the human person throughout his pontificate. In the case of Bergoglio, we find an added dimension that has something attractive about it.

What we should not fear, in fact, is not strong; it is light. It is not like iron, but rather it is as soft as a feather because Pope Francis says, "We should not be afraid of goodness, or better, of tenderness."

What does that mean? That we should lower our defenses, so as to live more peacefully? That we should seek harmony? He himself has taken the first step: always smiling, full of energy, generous, available.

And that "do not be afraid" (of goodness, of tenderness), with its expanded meaning, continues to reverberate throughout the Church.

E

18.

E IS FOR...EASTER

Every year at Christmas and at Easter, Fr. Bergoglio recorded an Easter message for TV on Channel 21. His last message was recorded just after the resignation of Benedict XVI and before he departed for the conclave in February 2013. It went on air on Wednesday, March 27, of Holy Week, after the election had taken place.

It is probably the shortest Easter message of any bishop or cardinal in Argentine history: just twenty-six seconds. We know that Bergoglio makes brevity one of his strong points, but this fact remains and it needs to be emphasized. What can you say in twenty-six seconds? Is it possible to launch a spiritual message in such a short time? Obviously, with Francis, the answer is yes. But, to give you an idea, this is what he said in that message:

No one has greater love than one who lays down his life for his friends. Jesus has done that for us, for you, for me. He won it back again and he accompanies us with his life, full of love. Let yourselves be accompanied by Jesus. He loves you. Easter is Jesus alive!

That was the end of the message to the Argentine nation, delivered in less than thirty seconds!

19.

E IS FOR..."EIGHTH SACRAMENT"

As we know, there are seven sacraments. But Pope Francis has discovered, in his experience as a parish priest and as a bishop, that some Catholic clergy seem to have invented an "eighth," which he refers to as the "Pastoral Customs House." He says this quite seriously, but the matter conceals a biting irony. To explain this, he tells the story of a girl we shall call Mary.

Mary is a single mother. She is alone and has many problems. She wants to have her child baptized. What does she do? She goes to the parish. She goes into the parish office and says, "I want to have my baby baptized."

Sitting at the desk there is one of the parish priest's helpers, who, quite unperturbed, gives her the answer: "No, you can't because you are not married."

At this point the pope can hardly contain his frustration. "But, look, this girl has had the courage to continue her pregnancy and what does she find? A closed door. This is not being zealous! Driving people away from the Lord! Not opening the doors! So, when we are like this, on this road, with this attitude, we do not do good for others, for people, for the People of God."

And the pope adds wryly, "Jesus instituted seven sacraments and we, with this attitude, we institute an eighth, the sacrament of the pastoral customs house."

20.

E IS FOR...EMOTIONS

Let's look once more at that unforgettable moment in history, March 13, 2013. Cardinal Tauran has the task of proclaiming the *Habemus Papam*. The formula has been the same for centuries; the only thing that changes is the name of the newly elected pope.

A few moments after the last phrase, *"Qui sibi nomen imposuit Franciscum,"* with a choreography that is perfect, the procession arrives and the new pope appears. At this point, try to enlarge the image in your mind.

Do you remember? Bergoglio arrives immobile, still, petrified. For one moment there is no movement of his head. No movement of his eyes. His hands are still. His mouth is closed. Then, into the microphone, he says, "Brothers and sisters." He stops. He raises his left hand. "Good evening." And he relaxes.

But what happens during those 30, 40, or 100 seconds in which he scarcely moves? What happened is what happens every time he experiences something very emotional. He freezes completely.

This happened on another March 13, in 1992. The apostolic nuncio of the time, Monsignor Ubaldo Calabresi, had made an appointment with him. At the end of the questioning, which Bergoglio states was very serious, he informed him that he was to become auxiliary bishop of Buenos Aires.

Bergoglio's reaction? "I was paralyzed." And he adds, "Whatever happens that is unexpected, good or bad, I am always the same. The first reaction is always negative."

F

21.

F IS FOR...FASTING

Every time I ask those who know him well whether Bergoglio is a man in the habit of fasting, the response is a thoughtful silence. The silence is of someone reflecting and who may even be trying to draw out a memory of some episode. For, if we reflect on it well, no one recalls him speaking about fasting, apart from at times proper to the Church's liturgy and calendar. At the same time, no one has ever seen him overdoing the eating of food. To be sure, he likes to cook and also to eat, but he has adopted as his own a style of moderation, of discretion, about which there would be much to write.

One example is at the celebration of Christmas. Every year at Christmas in Buenos Aires the future pope organized a meeting with journalists. He would give a few words about Jesus being born as a child, according to his rapid but very effective style, the offering of greetings, and then off to the buffet. And while the crowd milled around with the dishes in their hands, the cardinal, relaxed and smiling, would move around with just a glass of water, greeting and meeting people, chatting to them, dialoguing with them.

With just a glass of water for himself, he politely set people at their ease as he moved around in their midst as their pastor. This was the essence of Bergoglio.

22.

F IS FOR...FINGER

About a month and a half after his election, through the world's most popular social network, there arrived in Italy, duly translated, an Argentine prayer. The signature on it was that of Bergoglio. Prayer? Poetry? It was a little masterpiece of writing, worthy of a person of culture with a passion for literature. It showed the Jesuit cardinal's excellent ability with the pen. Here it is.

A Prayer for Every Finger of the Hand

The thumb is the finger closest to you. Begin praying, therefore, for those who are closest to you. These are the persons we recall most easily. Praying for those who are dear to us is a "pleasant duty."

The next finger is the index finger. Pray for those who teach, who educate, and who take care of people. This group includes teachers, professors, doctors, and priests. They need support and wisdom to point out the right way to others. Always remember them in your prayers.

The next finger is the longest or the highest. It makes us remember those who govern us. Pray for the president, the members of parliament, those who are employers and directors. These are the people who manage the destiny of our country and who guide public opinion....They need the guidance of God.

The fourth finger is the ring finger. It might surprise many of us, but this is our weakest finger, as any teacher of the pianoforte can confirm. It is there to remind us to pray for those who are the weakest among us, for those who have to face challenges, for the sick. They need your prayers day and night. We can never pray too much for them. And it is there also to invite us to pray for married couples.

And finally we arrive at the little finger, the smallest of all, as we should feel small before God and before our neighbor. As the Bible says, "The last shall be first." The little finger reminds you to pray for yourself....After you have prayed for everyone else, it will be at that point that you will be able to understand better what your own needs are, looking at them from the right perspective.

There is little to be added. I will say only that it has been published in a small booklet, with illustrations, and it has ended up being on the list of best-selling books in Italy. Perhaps, it is the first time that a prayer has leapt to the top of the charts.

23.

F IS FOR...FOOTBALL

On May 21, 2013, Juventus team captain Gianluigi (Gigi) Buffon is seated on a brown-colored sofa in the residence of St. Martha's. Beside him is the team's coach, Antonio Conte, whose eyes are fixed upon Pope Francis a few feet away. He is following with his eyes the lines the pope is drawing with his hands, and he is listening very closely to what the pope is saying.

"The other day," says the pope to the new champions of Italy, casually sitting around him, "passing by in a Jeep after the audience, I saw a man who greeted me with the jersey of San Lorenzo (the Argentine team that Bergoglio supported). I looked at him and I went like that." He holds up in the air his index, middle, and ring fingers, making "three." Then he closes his hand and reopens it straight-away, joining thumb and index finger in a "zero"—that is to say, "three–zero," the result by which San Lorenzo de Almagro had just beaten Boca in the Argentine derby just a few days before. They all burst out laughing, and the loudest laugh is the pope's.

Bergoglio has a tremendous passion for football (soccer). He has the season ticket number 88235N of San Lorenzo. The football team was founded almost a century ago by Fr. Lorenzo Massa with the purpose of helping the children of the streets play in a safe place. In the past San Lorenzo won many victories, and it still holds a respectable place in the First Division, the A series of the Argentine championship.

The day after his election, the pope was given a nickname by the Argentine sporting paper *Olé*. In huge letters he was called: *"La otra mano de Dios"* or "The other hand of God." Why the "other"? Well, football experts will already know why.

On June 22, 1986, in the Aztec stadium of Mexico City, in the fixtures of the World Cup a first-rate match took place between Argentina and England. Only four years had passed since the Falklands War. So there was an added dimension to this game of football.

In the second half, at 0–0, the king of Argentine football, Diego Armando Maradona, scores a crazy but astute goal, with a little bit of divine help, some say. "A bit with the head of Maradona and the other bit by the hand of God," Maradona himself will say after the match, laughing at his opponents, attributing to God and not to himself the move which sent the ball into the back of the net. But a few minutes after this hand-of-God goal, his majesty Maradona gets a ball in midfield. He jinks and dodges, flying past the entire English team, player after player. The goalkeeper comes out. Maradona goes around him too. He scores what the Fédération Internationale de Football Association (FIFA) has called "the greatest goal in the history of football."

The whole of Argentina, watching in front of the TV, explodes in jubilation. And who knows? Fr. Bergoglio must have been elated too. Led by Maradona, the Argentines reach the final and win the World Cup.

That title, "The other hand of God," then, is pure myth, history, pride. In the minds of the Argentines, God, football, and Argentina live in the same house. And in that house too, there is now also the pope.

Presently, Gigi Buffon stands up, holding in his hand jersey number one of Juventus, his own. It is autographed by the whole team. Handing it to the pope, Buffon proclaims, "To join you even more to Juve." Bergoglio smiles. No one there knows it at this time, but his mother, who was called Regina (Queen) Sivori, was related to the great Italo-Argentine Omar Sivori, who played for Juventus, the Bianconeri (the black-and-whites), and who was voted European Footballer of the Year in 1961.

24.

F IS FOR...FRANCIS

In the following account, three days after his election Francis explained to journalists how he chose his name. It is an account that is amusing, full of feeling, and at the same time very intense. It deserves to be presented in his own words:

During the election I had next to me the Emeritus Archbishop of São Paolo and Emeritus Prefect of the Congregation for the Clergy, Cardinal Claudio Hummes, a great friend, a great friend! When things began to look a bit dangerous, he gave me comfort. And when the votes rose to two-thirds, there was the usual applause, because the pope had been elected. Cardinal Hummes greeted me, he embraced me, and he said to me, "Don't forget the poor." And those words lodged into me here [tapping his head]: the poor, the poor. Then, straightaway, in connection with the poor, I thought of Francis of Assisi. Then, I thought about wars, while the voting continued until all the votes had been counted. And Francis was the man of peace. And so the name came to me, in my heart, Francis of Assisi. For me, he is the man of the poor, the man of peace, the man who loves and protects creation; at the present time, we don't have such a good relationship with creation, do we? He is the man who gives us this spirit of peace, this man of poverty….Ah, how I would like a Church which is poor and for the poor….I wish you all well. I thank you for all you have done.

In connection with this name, there is a request that Bergoglio made to the crowd on one occasion. On the afternoon of May 18, 2013, the pope was in St. Peter's Square for a meeting with associations of the laity, in the context of the Year of Faith. He made a very long tour in the white jeep and greeted everyone, and he in turn was greeted with great affection. But a little later, at the microphone, he makes the following appeal:

And now I would like to make a mild rebuke, in a brotherly way, just between us. You have all been calling out in the Square: "Francis, Francis, Pope Francis." But where was Jesus? I would have liked you to have shouted, "Jesus. Jesus is the Lord and he is really in our midst." From now on, no more Francis, but Jesus."

A great applause greeted this impromptu *motu proprio,* this unexpected papal oral command, but, to be honest about it, just a minute later, the people were shouting "Francis" once more.

25.

G IS FOR...GARMENTS

When Fr. Bergoglio became the archbishop of Buenos Aires, the person in the curia responsible for his clerical garments telephoned the tailor's to discover the cost of a new garment for the archbishop. He listened, made a note of the price in his notebook, promised to convey the tailor's regards to His Excellency, and, having thanked the tailor, ended the telephone call. He was not particularly concerned by the amount.

He went back to Fr. Bergoglio, who had been archbishop of Buenos Aires only a few days, and patiently waited his turn. To the Jesuit, his garments were not the most urgent problem, although they had told him he would need to dress in accordance with his rank. To whatever that expression might have meant, and the expression had not pleased him very much, he had replied, "Very well. Let's see what the price is."

"How much!" he exclaimed loudly, when the official showed him the sheet. "How much does it cost? We will never—and I mean *never*—spend that amount."

There followed various attempts to calm things down, to convince him, a lengthy and rather fruitless effort, when in the end he had a bright idea. "But where are the garments of Cardinal Quarracino?"

They looked for his garments in the wardrobe, examined them for size, but on the new Archbishop Bergoglio they were enormous.

"Could we call the sisters, please?" asked Bergoglio politely.

The sisters arrived, saw the problem, and smiled at one another. They took his measurements. They let in the material and shortened it, and the archbishop of Buenos Aires once more had his garments. They had cost nothing.

26.

G IS FOR...GESTURES (OF KINDNESS)

For Pope Francis the sign of power is tenderness.

His model for this is St. Joseph. Jesus's dad "appears as a man who is strong, courageous, a worker, but in his soul, there emerges a great tenderness, which is not the virtue of the weak; quite the opposite, it denotes strength of mind and a capacity for attending to people, compassion, real openness to others, a capacity for love. We should not be afraid of goodness, of tenderness."

We are no longer surprised when Francis embraces and kisses people on his tours in the popemobile. Such gestures of kindness can last for an hour.

It is no longer a surprise that the car leaves St. Peter's Square to enable the pope to see and to greet everyone. And no one is surprised when the car turns onto the Via della Conciliazione and even drives to the end of that road. And no one is too surprised when a woman, overcome with emotion at seeing the pope, drops her handbag. And no one should be surprised when he bends down to pick it up and give it back to her.

27.

G IS FOR...GIRLFRIEND

Yes, Jorge Mario Bergoglio was engaged. Who was he engaged to? Not much is known. Certainly she was part of the group of friends he used to go out dancing with. Perhaps he also had arranged to meet her on September 21, 1953, when he left home to meet his group of friends, and when, instead, he felt the need to go into a church and to go to confession. And there with a supernatural force that burst in upon him, he received the call of God to the priesthood. (See "V is for...Vocation" p. 140.)

But what happened after he had left his girlfriend and had entered into the seminary? That is very interesting. I will leave this extraordinary story to Bergoglio himself.

While I was a seminarian, I was bedazzled by a girl I had met at the wedding of one of my uncles. Her beauty, her acumen, struck me...and, well, I was confused for a good, long time; she turned my head. So, I went back to seminary, after the wedding, but I was unable to pray for an entire week because, every time I tried to compose myself for prayer, the picture of this girl kept appearing.

I had to rethink what I was doing. I was still free because I was a seminarian. I could return home and would have been well received. I had to rethink the choice I had made from the beginning. And I returned to choosing the path of the religious or rather of allowing myself to be chosen. There would be something wrong if these things did not happen. And, when they happen, you have to reflect upon what you are doing and where you are going. You have to see whether you should go back to the same choice or whether to say, "No; what I am trying out is very good, but I am afraid that I will not be faithful to my commitment; I will leave the seminary."

When something like this happens to a seminarian, I help him to leave in complete serenity, so that he may be a good Christian and not a bad priest.

28.

G IS FOR...GRANDMOTHER

G is indeed for Grandmother, the most important person in Bergoglio's life, according to him. Jorge grew up with his grandmother, Rosa, while his mother and his father took care of their second son, who was born quite soon after him.

Grandmother Rosa is a woman of deep spirituality, capable of capturing the attention of her grandchildren when she is speaking of Jesus. The pope received the first proclamation of the Christian message from her, through her actions, her words, and her devotions.

Each year on Good Friday she took her grandchildren to the procession with candles. At the appearance of the statue of the crucified Christ, she made the children genuflect and say, "Look. He is dead. But tomorrow he will rise again."

When Jorge decided to become a priest, his grandmother pretended to be surprised, but she had already understood it all in her heart. Her reassuring words, which the pope keeps to this day in his *Liturgy of the Hours,* he kept close to him during the years in the seminary. During the time when Bergoglio's mother was closed in, in a mute nonacceptance of his vocation, his grandmother's words supported his choice, but reminded him that the door to her house was always open, if he decided to turn back. (See also "I is for...Inheritance," p. 70.)

H

29.

H IS FOR...HÖLDERLIN

Friedrich Hölderlin is the poet Bergoglio appreciates most. He has defined the German poet as "a great master of nostalgia." Hölderlin lived until 1843 and is regarded as one of the greatest exponents of European Romanticism.

This must have provoked a certain degree of pride among Germans. Chancellor Merkel, on an official visit after the election of March 13, 2013, had the very good idea of giving a present to the new pontiff: an original 1905 edition of Hölderlin in three volumes. As she handed them to him, she proclaimed with Teutonic pride, "You are a connoisseur of Hölderlin." The pope could do no other than confirm this.

30.

H IS FOR...HOLIDAY

Did Bergoglio ever go on holiday, even as cardinal? No, never. When he was rector of the Maximo College, so his ex-pupils have recounted, his holiday was to stay in peace at the college "without the boys, who had gone home." He relaxes by praying and by being with people. He is happy doing that and doesn't need anything else. He is a man of God, but to understand this, we need to understand the people of Argentina.

The Argentine people do not have holidays. Therefore, if you want to be one of them, even if you are a cardinal, out of respect for others, do not go on holiday. To be sure, if you want to go into the mountains for a fortnight, no one would be scandalized, but in Argentina, people work sixteen hours a day, from Sunday to Sunday. It is said, "If you have a job, God be blessed; you must work."

One day Bergoglio said, "The Jesuits have the vow of poverty among their vows, don't they? Very good. And what does the poor man do? He has to work. Have you taken a vow of poverty? All right; then you must work."

31.

H IS FOR...HOMILIES

Bergoglio has invented a new way of being pope—to be a parish priest. The morning Mass is no longer private or restricted. Francis celebrates every day in front of a group. That is new. There are also television cameras, which then transmit a summary of his words. This means that every day, in the simplicity of a chapel that was not built for a pope, Francis communicates messages about good Christian living or opens the door on a very special school of prayer.

Francis speaks without a text. He gives a commentary on the day's reading, extracting from it a small-message-that-is-never-small and that each one can, so to say, put in a bag and take away as an inspiration for the day.

Sometimes he repeats himself. He knows that and says so because the model of his preaching is that of rain wearing away at rock. It is the biblical certainty that the Word does not get lost. The homily at St. Martha's is like a seed: small, hidden, constant, simple. From that small chapel, the pope takes the world by the hand.

32.
H is for...Humility

The telephone in the office of the archbishop of Buenos Aires was always ringing. Often those who rang were men and women who claimed to have received "a gift from God." Which gifts? Prophecies, healings, messages to be spread.

Bergoglio knows that the history of the Church is marked by these gifts, and it does not surprise him to get these calls. But he has identified a way to flush out the cheats and the overexcited. When these people are humble, the gifts come from God. But, if in the place of humility there is vanity, pride, or a tendency toward turning everything into a spectacular event, then God has got nothing to do with it and it is a pretext for making money.

Bergoglio has learned that humility is the path toward God. And this lesson needs to be learned, avoiding gossip and complaints. Humility. It is not by accident, therefore, that on TV, when asked what most strikes them about Bergoglio, people's first response is: "His humility."

33.
I IS FOR...IMAGES

Whether it is because of his love for literature and for the arts or his habit of reading, what is certain is that Pope Francis definitely knows how to use words. He has the gift of inventing images and of constructing metaphors that are at one and the same time elegant and popular, rich in meaning, and easy to recall. Among the many in existence, I put forward ten, each one a subject for meditation.

A caress in the night: "In the middle of the night of the many 'nights' of so many sins which we commit, there is always that caress of the Lord, which seems to say, 'This is my glory.'"

Tears are spectacles: "At some times in life, the spectacles for seeing Jesus are our tears. We cry over what is good, over our sins, for the grace we receive, for joy. Let us ask ourselves, have we had that happiness of tears which prepares our eyes to look upon and to see the Lord?"

Our Lady's garments: "Let us pray to Our Lady, that she may protect us; in times of spiritual upset, the safest place is within the folds of her garments."

The Church as babysitter: "Proclaim Jesus with our life; when we do this the Church becomes a mother Church, who generates children; but, when we do not do this, the Church becomes not a mother, but a babysitter, who looks after the child to get him or her to go to sleep. It is a soothing Church. Let us think about the responsibility which comes from our baptism."

A "spray god": "In what God do you believe? A 'god spread around'? A 'spray god' who somehow is a bit all over the place, but you do not know what he really is? We believe in God who is Father, who is Son, who is Holy Spirit. We believe in Persons, and when we pray to God, we pray to Persons; either I pray to the Father or I pray to the Son or I pray to the Holy Spirit. And this is the faith."

A confessional is an encounter with Jesus: "The confessional is not the dry-cleaner's; it is an encounter with Jesus, with that Jesus who is waiting for us, who is waiting for us as we are. 'But, Lord, Listen, I am so...'—but we feel ashamed to speak the truth: "I have done this, I have thought that..." But shame is an authentic Christian virtue and a human virtue too...the capacity to feel ashamed. I do not know whether in Italian you say this, but in our country, of those who cannot feel shame, they say; "*sin verguenza*" or "shameless." He is someone who is "shameless" because he does not have the capacity to feel shame and being ashamed is a virtue of the humble, of that man or of that woman who is humble."

Mr. Moaner: "When difficulties arise, many temptations appear also. For example, the temptation to complain, 'But, just look what has happened to me ...' A moan. And a Christian who is always complaining ceases to be a good Christian; they become Mr. or Mrs. Moaner, don't they? Because they always moan about everything, don't they? Silence in suffering; silence in patience. That is the silence of Jesus. In his passion, Jesus did not speak much, only two or three words which were necessary.... But apart from that, it is not a sad silence; the silence of suffering the cross is not a sad silence. It is painful, many times it is very painful, but it is not sad. His heart is at peace. Paul and Silvanus prayed in peace. They suffered pain, because we are told that the prison officer washed their wounds—they had wounds—but they suffered them in peace. This path of suffering enables us to deepen that peace which is Christian; it makes us strong in Christ."

Peppered vinegar: "If we want to have this joy just for ourselves, in the end we become ill and our heart becomes a bit crumpled, and our face no longer transmits that great joy, but rather a melancholy, that is no longer healthy. Sometimes such melancholy Christians have faces that are more like peppered vinegar than the faces of people who are joyful and who have a good life. Joy cannot be halted; it must go forward."

Museum Christians: "Salt has meaning when it is used to give taste to things. I think also that salt kept in a bottle loses its power with the humidity and is no longer any use. Through the adoration of the Lord and through the proclamation of the Gospel, I go out of myself to give the message. But, if we do not do this, the salt will remain in the bottle and we will become Christians in a museum. We can let the salt be seen. This is my salt. But how beautiful it is! This is the salt I received in baptism, this is what I received in confirmation, this is what I received through catechesis…but, look, museum Christians. 'If salt has lost its taste…it is no longer good for anything.'"

The lights of the Olympic Stadium: "Reality, which at times is dark and marked by evil, can change, if in the first place we bring to it the light of the Gospel, especially by the lives we live. If on a dark night in a stadium—here in Rome we can think of the Olympic Stadium or of that of San Lorenzo in Buenos Aires—if a person lights a lamp, you would hardly be able to see it, but if the other seventy thousand spectators each light their own lamp, the whole stadium is illuminated. Let us act in such a way that our life becomes a light of Christ; together, let us bring the light of the Gospel to the whole of reality."

34.

I IS FOR...INHERITANCE

The good feelings and the sacred values of the Gospel are the inheritance that Jorge Mario Bergoglio has received from his family. And it is obvious that the most valuable inheritance he received came from his grandmother, Rosa—the most important person in Pope Francis's life as reported by Francesca Ambrogetti.

Money? No. To be able to see the inheritance he received, you need to go to *The Liturgy of the Hours,* the book that Bergoglio, like every priest, holds in his hands several times a day. To this day, between pages of the psalms and the readings, the pope keeps some letters and the will of his grandmother. Here is a section that he has made public:

That my grandchildren, to whom I have given the best of myself, may have a long and happy life. But, if some day sadness, sickness, or the loss of a loved one should fill them with sorrow, that they should always remember that a sigh before the Tabernacle, where the greatest and most glorious martyr is kept, and a gaze upon Mary at the foot of the cross can cause a drop of balsam to fall upon the deepest and most painful of wounds.

35.

I IS FOR...ISOLAMENTE

"Why is it that you... you have given up all the riches of a pope, such as his luxury apartment, and have gone to live in a small flat nearby?" asks a female student of the Leo XIII College. They are at a meeting of schools organized by the Jesuits on June 7, 2013.

"For psychiatric reasons," is the extraordinary and penetrating reply. Francis adds, "It is my personality. Besides, the apartment [in the Apostolic Palace] is not so luxurious; it is not a major issue....But I cannot live on my own, if you understand me? It is not a question of me being personally virtuous; it is simply that I cannot live on my own."

Let's try to put together, then, the different elements of Bergoglio's personality. He does not have secretaries, he does not want people working for him, he does not want to be driven around, and in Argentina he goes around on his own. Bergoglio has always sought a certain degree of solitude and, indeed, he has managed to win this for himself. After all, there are many who would have wanted to be part of his, let us call it, "court." But he has rejected the idea of a court. And so? And so, it is not so much the idea of solitude that frightens him. Indeed, he lives the life almost of a monk.

The correct word in Italian is another one: *isolamento* ("isolation"). That is what he fears. And not because something might happen to him, but because a priest, even if he is the pope, cannot live in a glass bubble, shielded from everything. "Or at least, that is not my personality," he says.

36.

I IS FOR...ITALIAN

Though his family emigrated from Italy, Jorge Bergoglio was not born in Italy; he is 100 percent Argentine. Still, he has a surprising way of defining himself: "I am the most Italian of my family." What does this mean? To explain this, we need to enter into the house of his grandparents, who took care of little Jorge from the time he was only thirteen months of age, because his mother was pregnant with another child.

It was here in his grandparents' home that Jorge will attend the most important school of humanity and of theology of his life, that of his grandmother Rosa. It will also be the most profound school of Italian and of "Italianness" that could be imagined.

Listening to his grandmother and grandfather, Jorge even learns the Piedmontese dialect. While for his father Italy is a source of sadness, with his grandparents, everything will be much calmer. (In practical terms, it was almost impossible to talk to his father about Italy, as each time there was not just a refusal, but a sort of running away, as if leaving his fatherland was still a bleeding wound.)

Words, traditions, culture: Bergoglio drinks it all in like mother's milk. If to this we add that he learned the Italian language at home with his parents and add his love for Italian films, it emerges that the Argentine pope is also an Italian pope—but he is a "pasta" that is no longer to be found in Italy. It is the Italy of seventy years ago, with fewer big cities and with more heart. The image of the Italy that echoes back from Latin America is in stark contrast to the present years of educational crisis. It is an image that seems at times beyond recognition.

37.

J IS FOR...JESUIT

Why did Bergoglio decide to enter the Jesuits, leaving the diocesan seminary after a year? Because he was conquered by the image of the advance guard, by the missionary spirit of which the Society of Jesus were (and still are) justly proud.

The young Jorge wanted to be a missionary. And wasn't Francis Xavier, patron of missionaries, a Jesuit? In this way, almost seeing himself in the steps of Francis Xavier, when he was studying theology, Bergoglio takes pen and paper and writes to the General—namely, to the priest who at that time was the head of the Society of Jesus, Fr. Pedro Arrupe. He asks to be sent to Japan.

Fr. Arrupe reflects for a few days and then replies. Bergoglio recounts:

> Fr. Arrupe thought it over and said to me, "But you have had a lung disease; that is not a good

thing for such demanding work as this." And so I stayed in Buenos Aires. But Fr. Arrupe had been good because he did not say: "You are not holy enough to become a missionary"; he was good, he had charity.

Fr. Bergoglio jokes about it, but it was a hard blow. He went immediately to kneel before the Blessed Sacrament. He asked the Lord why he had put into his heart a desire that could not be fulfilled for reasons of health. Where was the sense in that? His burden made him think of the burden of St. Thérèse of Lisieux. She is a patron of missionaries. She, too, desired to go on the missions but was unable to do so for reasons of health—a story with a parallel to his own. And, in fact, he has a great devotion to that saint, as we shall see.

Meanwhile, though, as to his shattered dreams about Japan, this is one of the things about which he jokes most easily. "There are people here in Argentina who would have been saved from me if I had gone to Japan, isn't that right?"

38.
K is for...Kisses

It is Sunday morning on June 2, 2013. On the Via dei Fori Imperiali in Rome, everything is ready for the military parade. The vehicles of the city's street-cleaning services pass by for the last time to clean the road. The road signs that have just been renovated are being polished. There is a lot of noise. The preparations are frantic.

A few hundred meters away as the crow flies, in the chapel of the residence of St. Martha in the Vatican, there is, in contrast, a profound silence. Eighty people, anxious and excited, are awaiting the pope for Mass. For the most part they are relatives of members of the Italian military services who died on peace missions, but there are also thirteen Italian military personnel who had been wounded. Their names were heard on television news reports after various attacks in recent years in Afghanistan, names that have been forgotten.

The pope arrives, walking at a slow pace. The Mass begins.

During the homily he has harsh words against war: "It is madness," he proclaims. "It is the suicide of the human race." After the blessing he wants to greet everyone one by one. He approaches a young man, strong but stuck in his wheelchair. Sitting there without any legs at all, he looks up at Bergoglio and bursts into tears. Before the eyes of this thirty-year-old pass all the episodes of violence he has seen and the sorrow he has witnessed, and they are mixed with the dear, white figure of Pope Francis.

The pope bends down to him.

Another young man follows. He is bigger than the pope, and has one eye in bandages. The other good eye is pouring with tears. They embrace each other. The pope caresses his face with his hand and they exchange a kiss on the cheek.

A pope who allows himself to be kissed?

Yes. That is how he is. He kisses his friends during the audiences. He even gave a kiss to the Argentine president, Christine Fernandez de Kirchner. He kisses countless numbers of children at the audiences on Wednesdays. In one case, when a child was crying, Francis simply took the pacifier dangling around the child's stomach and put it in his mouth.

Often, greeting crowds from the popemobile, he raises his right or left thumb, like Fonzie. Then he throws kisses with his hand. "Don't be afraid of tenderness," he said one day. And he does not limit himself just to saying it.

39.
L IS FOR...LAITY

What Fr. Bergoglio thinks of the laity is well represented by a story he often likes to tell. It is set in Japan where, in the seventeenth century, a bloody persecution of Christians meant all the priests were driven away or killed.

For two hundred years Japan remained without priests. Yet, when they returned, the missionaries did not find, as they had feared, communities that were lost or abandoned, but "everything in place, everyone baptized, everyone catechized, everyone married in church." For two hundred years, without priests, the faith had been maintained thanks to the baptized, the laypeople who provided continuity and an exemplary transmission of the faith.

It was also for this reason that in the Villas Miserias of Buenos Aires, Fr. Bergoglio entrusted so much work to the laypeople. But, beware! "Clericalism is a problem," he warns. "Priests clericalize the laity and the laity ask to be clericalized."

40.

M IS FOR…MARY

It is 8:30 a.m. on March 14, 2013. For a little more than twelve hours, the Catholic Church has had a new pope. The news offices are still in confusion when an agency news flash makes it clear what the atmosphere is like and what kind of pontificate it will be. The pope is on his way back from the basilica of St. Mary Major. This in itself is not an item of news. Pope Francis himself had given an advance signal of it the night before from the balcony of St. Peter's Square, saying that he would be going to pray to Our Lady.

If anything, the news is something else—namely, that at the time when the editions were still being printed, the pope had already been there and prayed. From this we discover that Bergoglio is a morning man who takes little sleep. It remains the case that, very early, and as the first real act of his pontificate, Pope Francis wanted to go to pray to the Mother of God.

Bergoglio has a great devotion to Mary, particularly Our Lady of Luján, the Madonna of the Argentines, a figure that recalls the Virgin of Loreto (even if the wood is colored white). Our Lady of Luján also recalls the Virgin of Pompeii because her feast is celebrated on May 8, the day of prayer in the region of Campania. Fr. Bergoglio never missed that feast day at the shrine where every year a million young people gather, exhausted, at the end of pilgrimage.

Bergoglio also often visited the little church of Our Lady of Caacupé, the Madonna of the Villas Miserias (Misery Villages), whose white-walled church rises up among the huts of the shantytowns on the outskirts of Buenos Aires.

And then there is the Madonna who unties knots: Mary, Untier of Knots (*Maria Als Knotenlöserin*). Fr. Bergoglio studied theology for a time in Germany where he came to know this beautiful devotion and took it back with him to Argentina. Nowadays, it is one of the most widespread devotions in the country. And during the days of the novena, recited by so very many people, the Argentines cannot but think of the man who had made it known to them.

41.

M IS FOR…MERCY

Mercy is the word Pope Francis uses most. At the heart of his teaching is the idea that God never tires of forgiving. A woman of advanced years, who wanted to go to confession, had once made this very point to him. He himself related the story on the Sunday of his first Angelus.

> Bergoglio: But, if you haven't committed any sins …
> Woman: All of us have committed sins…but the Lord forgives everything.
> Bergoglio: How do you know that?
> Woman: If the Lord didn't forgive everything, the world would not exist.
> Bergoglio: Tell me, have you studied at the Gregorian? Because that is the wisdom that is given by the Holy Spirit, the interior wisdom about the mercy of God. Let's not forget these words: The Lord never tires of forgiving us, never. The problem is that we grow tired; we don't want to ask, we grow tired of asking for forgiveness. He does not grow tired of forgiving us, but at times we grow tired of asking him for forgiveness.

The pope then coined a new and very significant phrase: "The science of tenderness."

42.

M IS FOR...MIGRANTS

Why did the Bergoglio family decide to leave Portacomaro to emigrate to Argentina? Money problems? At the beginning of 1929, the year of the Great Depression, the financial crisis brought the world's economy to its knees. Millions of Italians emigrated because of famine. But not the Bergoglios. They left for reasons of affection and tenderness, values that in future in the pope's homilies would capture the attention of the whole world. These values the pope would cite as being fundamental. Yes, they leave for reasons of affection and tenderness.

In Argentina, in fact, three of the six brothers of Grandfather Giovanni had already arrived and, even though it meant leaving two other brothers in Italy, Francis's grandfather decided to join them. Therefore, Grandfather Giovanni and Grandmother Rosa sold their pastry shop and the other few goods they had, and with what they gained from the sale, boarded the Giulio Cesare (Julius Caesar).

Bergoglio always recounts two family stories. The first is that he would not even have been born had it not been for the unforeseen delays that followed the plan for the sale of the pastry shop. Had it not been for those delays, in fact, the Bergoglios would have left before 1929 and would have taken a cabin on the Princess Mafalda, the liner that had been the pride of the Italian Navy, but which fractured in 1927 off the shores of Brazil (almost at the end of the crossing from Genoa to Buenos Aires) with the loss of more than three hundred lives. In Grandfather Giovanni's pockets were the unused tickets for this liner. There was a time when many Italian emigrants drowned off the shores, on their way to their new home. On July 8, 2013, Francis threw a bouquet of flowers into the waters of Lampedusa to recall the recent African refugees who had died en route as well as all the victims of every migration in the history of the human race.

The other story concerns his grandmother. Rosa hid all the money, the fruit of the sale they had made in Piedmont, in the hem of her overcoat, which she kept tightly around her throughout the voyage. It is a pity that, when they alighted onto Argentine soil, it was January— yes, but January in the Southern Hemisphere, which is summer in Latin America. Not the best time, certainly, for an overcoat.

The pope loves to tell these stories, for they remind him of his Italian roots. He knows the Piedmontese dialect very well and does not hesitate to call himself "the most Italian of his family" (see "I is for...Italian," p. 73).

43.

M IS FOR...MIRACLES (OF BERGOGLIO)

The newsagent was waiting for Fr. Bergoglio with a special smile. It was December 19, 1985. He had put aside a copy of *El Litoral* and hoped that the Jesuit would not see the posters hanging outside. Yes, because that morning, there really was something to laugh about.

"Fr. Bergoglio's Miracles," proclaimed the headline of one paper. Miracles? What miracles? Bergoglio was the parish priest of St. Joseph's and the rector of the Maximo College. For five years he had committed himself fully, it is true, but *miracle* is a big word.

And so, when he arrived at the newsagent's, before his eyes was the last remaining copy of the daily, with that headline. Very much struck, he read the article.

The first miracle recognized by the papers as Bergoglio's was the opening of two churches in one of the most forgotten quarters of the northeast of Buenos Aires.

The second miracle: two more churches were planned.

The third miracle, as reported by the paper, was that social activities were being planned for families and for the children of the area, who, so wrote the paper, "no longer seemed to be the angry people who, until very recently, welcomed outsiders by throwing stones at them."

The fourth miracle was the opening of the biggest library of theology and of philosophy in the whole of Latin America, that of the Maximo College.

And finally, the fifth miracle: an international theological congress.

The comments made by the future pope after reading this article were no doubt very incisive. Unfortunately they are not available to us.

44.

M IS FOR...MISTAKE

What is the Argentine pope's most frequent mistake, his most recurrent error? It is he himself who tells us. It is no accident that this was on the occasion when he visits Casal del Marmo, the young persons' prison in Rome, where he celebrates the Holy Thursday Mass in 2013. Needing to give an example, he makes known his own defect.

Speaking himself but not about himself, he says, "Sometimes, I am a bit annoyed with one person or another.... Let it be and, if they ask you a favor, do it...." He says this to the young offenders detained there. He was about to wash and kiss the feet of twelve of them, repeating Jesus's act to his apostles at the Last Supper.

It was certainly good advice to give, but he also recognizes his own shortcomings in this area. "I am not always understanding and just, and this hurts me," he declares.

Every morning, Pope Francis prays that he may obtain what Pope John XXIII called "wisdom of heart"—that is to say, to know how to be able to deal with people and situations. Then, facing a problem, with the candor of a child, he reveals, "I made a mistake, I acted badly, and I have to turn back and apologize."

A bishop's responsibility is heavy. He has to coordinate, guide, and make decisions about people. He has to exercise authority. But Bergoglio admits that his mistakes have helped him because they help him to understand the mistakes of others.

45.

M IS FOR...MONEY

Celebrations for the newly elected Argentine pope were underway in the Plaza de Mayo, the heart of Buenos Aires, which sits between the Casa Rosada, the seat of the government, and the cathedral. The Apostolic Nuncio to Buenos Aires, Monsignor Emil Paul Tscherrig, was the bearer of news that could have been like a cold shower to all except the Argentines.

After speaking to the pope, the Nuncio signed a letter addressed to the bishops and archbishops, and through them to the whole country. The letter, in Francis's name, states two points very clearly.

First, thank you for the prayers, the good wishes and the affection which you have shown.

Secondly, the pope asks you a favor: Please don't travel to the Mass for the beginning of his pontificate. Instead of "going to Rome" (*"en lugar de ir a Roma"*) continue in your spiritual closeness, "accompanying it with a gesture of charity toward those who are most in need" (*"accompañandola con algun gesto de caridad hacia los más necesitados"*). In short, don't come to Rome, and give what you would have spent on travel to the poor.

Amazed? In Argentina no one is surprised. And not

only because Bergoglio had made the same request in 2001, when he was created cardinal by John Paul II, but because everyone knows what he thinks about money.

He has never wanted to travel in first class. When they asked him to move up because there were spare seats, he preferred to stay in second class. If it happened that someone made arrangements for him, and purchased a business-class ticket, he would go back to ask them to change it. He is not in favor of pauperism; he just does not want privileges, and since he is aware of so much poverty, he wants to be able to help the greatest number of people possible.

Fr. Bergoglio is not hostile to private property, but he is opposed to the flight of capital abroad. He asks: How can you produce wealth in a country, through the workers who must live in that country, and then displace the accumulated capital?

Money has its homeland. When I ask, before a debate, whether everyone pays taxes, many reply, "No, because the State is a robber and I give the money instead to the poor." These are justifications for failing to fulfill a duty.... I never accept the restitution of money which has been earned immorally [through dirty or fraudulent gains], unless those concerned are really penitent, otherwise, they wipe clear their conscience and then continue their criminal activities."

46.

M IS FOR...MOTHER

So far Regina, the pope's mother, has been described as someone with whom Bergoglio did not immediately share the discovery of his vocation. It took years before she could accept that vocation. But that desperate embrace between her and her son in the hospital is proof of an intense and strong relationship between them (see also "S is for...Sickness," p. 124).

Regina is a beautiful woman: reassuring, happy, smiling. A good woman. She, like his father, Mario, is of Italian origin. It is she who passed to their five children a love for the opera. She used to gather them around the radio, explaining the plot beforehand and the various passages of the works. That was something wonderful, according to Bergoglio. And, no doubt, there was something of the memory of his mother, Regina, in that gesture that his boys at the Maximo College still recall, when, waving the tickets in his hands, he would accompany them to the theater where they would listen to opera and learn from its depths.

47.

M IS FOR...MOTTO

Miserando atque eligendo: "By showing mercy and by choosing [us]." This was the motto used by Monsignor Bergoglio as bishop. This is the motto he has kept since his election as pope. He took it from a homily of St. Bede the Venerable on the call of St. Matthew. Caravaggio has depicted this event masterfully in *The Calling of St. Matthew*, which can be seen in Rome in the church of San Luigi dei Francesi (St. Louis of the French).

In this passage from St. Bede from which he took his motto—Looking upon us out of his mercy and choosing us—Bergoglio rediscovered himself when he was living through that explosive and supernatural event, the call to the priesthood. But *mercy* is also the word Pope Francis uses most in his homilies and in his speeches. His motto, therefore, is a snapshot of his vocation and of his magisterium.

48.
N IS FOR...NGO

No! The Church is not an NGO (Non-Governmental Organization), not even one which is praiseworthy, which does good things and saves people. Even if the Church is all of this and does all of this, it is not all that she is. This is one of the thoughts that Francis has most at heart.

An NGO is an organization, an office, involving people who work to implement a plan. The Church, Francis once said, is instead a story of love in which we participate and in which being efficient is not what matters. Offices are important, but they are not essential in the Church, since what is of value in the Church is preaching the Gospel and giving witness to the faith.

49.
O IS FOR...OLIVOS

Up until February 28, 1998, the day on which Bergoglio was appointed archbishop of Buenos Aires, his predecessors lived in a magnificent residence about twelve miles from the cathedral and from the curia. It was a quiet place, elegant, a bit outside of the city, in an area called Olivos, a few steps away from the house of the president of the Republic. Yes, in Buenos Aires the temporal power and the religious power lived comfortably and close to each other, in one of the most prestigious areas of the suburbs.

Then Bergoglio arrived.

He had never wanted to go to the residence in Olivos—too reserved, too aristocratic, too far from the people. He chose to stay in the curia, a few steps away from the Plaza de Mayo—the heart of Buenos Aires where the whole city flows by, rushes around, and struggles, and it is good to know that your bishop is there, with you.

"I stay in the heart of the city because I have the city in my heart" could have been the slogan to represent that choice. The result was that lines of women and men, as though drawn by a light, began to cross this threshold and to leave messages or cards for him, trying to approach him or to have a word with him.

Even when he had been vicar general in Flores, it had been like that. He had taken up residence in the humblest of rooms, a bed, a table, a bookcase, a crucifix, some statues—among which St. Joseph stood out. Computer? There wasn't one. TV? Not even that.

In Buenos Aires, though, aside from his bedroom, he needed to choose an office. There was a large reception room, already furnished, with wooden seats and red covers, windows, curtains. Next to it, there was a small, undecorated room, with a table, a half-empty bookcase, and a chair. Does Fr. Bergoglio choose the furnished reception-room office or the undecorated room? I think there is no need to say. You can guess.

50.

P IS FOR...PARISH

In Italian, *P* is also for pastor, flock, combing, and smelling. Why is this important? Because the image in which Bergoglio is completely immersed, mystically immersed, is the biblical image of the Good Shepherd who goes in search of the single lost sheep and leaves the ninety-nine who are in the sheepfold.

He once said that parish priests must have the smell of their sheep (exactly that—smell) because when they take the wounded, lost, tired animals on their shoulders, they become impregnated with their odor, and so it must be!

On another occasion, he warned parish priests and parishes that they must not waste time combing the sheep, putting curlers into their hair (that is exactly what he said). This means that parish priests should not only concern themselves with guarding the faithful who have been pleased to stay or who have the good fortune to remain in the sheepfold. Combing the sheep's wool takes up time needed for searching for those sheep that are in danger.

When he speaks about parishes, Bergoglio demonstrates all of his pastoral understanding. According to a sociological study that ended up on the archbishop of Buenos Aires's desk, the area of influence of a parish in an area of the city generally extends up to six hundred meters (about half a mile). But parishes in Argentina are established more than a mile apart from each other. Therefore, if a block of flats is in a sense only a meter outside of this six-hundred-meter area, the people in that block (and farther) may have no perception of the parish's presence and of its activities. And, as a result, that block of flats is as if it had been abandoned.

The archbishop of Buenos Aires decided to invite the priests to hire out garages [on the edges of their parish boundaries] so they could conduct certain parish activities with the help of laypeople, rather like a small branch of the parish. Many parish priests were scandalized at this proposal and objected: "But, if we do that, they won't come to the parish."

And Bergoglio replied, "What? You mean that they come now?"

Almost instinctively, those parish priests responded, "No." Bergoglio avoided drawing the inference. They had given the answer themselves.

51.

P IS FOR...PARISH PRIEST

In 1980, forty-four-year-old Bergoglio had a very important experience. At the same time as being appointed rector of the Maximo College in St. Michael's diocese in the province of Buenos Aires, he was also appointed parish priest of St. Joseph's, at the back of the college. St. Joseph's is a poverty-stricken area full of huts.

For the students who were future Jesuits priests, observing their rector will be one of the most valuable experiences they gain: "He always pressed us to go into the midst of the people," they tell me today, thirty years later. "He used to say to us: Go into the streets and look for children who need their catechism; stay with the sick, go and visit them. It is true, you are not yet priests, you are not doctors, you are not nurses. You cannot even bring them an aspirin. But you must be with them. You must live in their midst."

That is what he did, exactly as he does today. He liked living in the midst of the people, and he did it without any demonstration of an attitude of authority, without anyone escorting him there, without barriers, with simplicity.

"When we were ordained priests, the people used to say that it seemed that we had always been priests. And you know why? Because, in accordance with Fr. Bergoglio's will, we never stayed locked within the college but were always on the streets, among the old, the children, the workers, among the dogs and the mud. They called us brothers. And when for the first time we sat in a confessional, we heard the sufferings we had known for years."

And Bergoglio, how was he as a parish priest? Exactly as he is now, only everything about him now seems fuller and more mature. And even those who know him well find it hard to explain how that is so.

52.

P IS FOR...PATIENCE

Is it possible to describe Pope Francis in a single word? I will try to suggest one: the pope of patience. Young people, he recognizes, rightly feel the urgent need to change the world. But, very quickly, as they grow up, they discover that this objective is unattainable if they are in a hurry. It can only be done with patience. This is something that parents know well when they understand that, beyond giving a model of life to their children, they must just learn to wait until the child makes his or her own life and, if need be, his or her own mistakes.

One of Bergoglio's best-loved passages of the Gospel is that of the merciful father in the Parable of the Prodigal Son. It is the passage in which the son wants to receive his inheritance. He then goes away and sinks to the very bottom of existence, and then he returns home. And the father? He sees him coming home, a sign that he was "standing at the window, in other words, waiting for him," the pope explains.

To make himself better understood, the pope speaks of a kite, which, as it turns, begins to tremble. At that point instinct would make you pull the cord, to take back control. But that would be a mistake. When the kite "wags its tail," you must give—let it have its way; you must set it free (without abandoning it), you must give it time. We could call it the Gospel of Patience.

53.

P IS FOR...PIGS

There are no photographs, but the testimony of the lads from the Maximo College is worth more than a photo. In the years when Bergoglio was rector, the college had a pigsty full of pigs. Each day, it was necessary to bring them food and water. The lads looked after this, on the basis of weekly shifts, but every day, literally dirtying his hands, sinking his feet into the mud, and facing what was no small effort, there was also the rector himself.

There was no humble work from which Bergoglio exempted himself or that he did not share with his boys. They still recall this today. "He never gave an order and sat there and watched. He gave us an example, getting his hands dirty."

54.

P IS FOR...POLITICS

As a youth Bergoglio was very interested in politics. He never took an active part in politics, but he read a lot about it, especially two reviews that were edited by the Communist party, *Nuestro Palabra* and *Propositos*. He makes it clear, though, that he was never a communist. Nor did he take part in politics as a bishop, even if he did not stay quiet when he was aware of sufferings, slavery, and the injustices that afflicted the poor. But that is first and foremost a matter of the Gospel: "Involving themselves in politics for Christians is a duty," he said to a young student at one of the Jesuit schools two months after the election. "We Christians cannot play at being Pilate, washing our hands. True, politics is often dirty, but I ask myself, why is it dirty? Is it because Christians do not involve themselves in it, in the spirit of the Gospel?"

55.

P IS FOR...PRAYER

How does the pope pray? How much does he pray? Those who know him consider him to be a man who is totally captivated by God in prayer. Before liturgical celebrations, we see him engrossed, seated there, with a thoughtful expression on his face; already he is completely in the Lord.

After Mass, if he can, he goes to the back seat and continues in silent prayer. He sleeps little, not more than five hours a night, and he gets up early. His first hours are spent before the Blessed Sacrament. Sometimes he has fallen asleep on the prie-dieu, but he does not make an issue of it. Part of his daily rule is the Liturgy of the Hours, the first and the last action of every day.

In the middle of the day there is the rosary. He has never been afraid of popular devotions. He himself practices a number of them, and he has spread many of these devotions, among which one is to the Madonna who unties knots, Mary Untier of Knots. For him prayer is not a matter of reciting formulae but of encountering God. And in this sense he has given a wonderful definition of what is happening when he prays: "It is as if God is holding me by the hand."

56.
Q IS FOR...QUOTES

Whom does the pope like to quote? He can often be heard quoting now this author, now that one, as people do with great philosophers or writers. But is he also knowledgeable about music, literature, the cinema? Does he watch television? Does he listen to the radio? What about the Internet? Let's take things in order.

As we have said, he has a great passion for books. He also likes classical music, the tango, the milonga. As a youngster, he liked dancing. It does not look as if there was a television set in his room in Argentina. To keep himself informed, Pope Francis prefers reading newspapers. He used to buy them personally from his newsagent. Up to now he has not mentioned any great passion for the new technologies or for the Internet.

On the other hand, as a child he used to go with his siblings to the local cinema, where they used to show up to three films a day. He is an expert on the cinema. His parents took him to see Anna Magnani and Aldo Frabrizi, and he has remained an admirer of neorealism. His favorite film is *Babette's Feast*.

Answering questions in the Paul VI audience hall to a child who asked him if he had ever been to Sicily, he revealed that he owed his knowledge of that region to a film of the Taviani brothers, called *Kaos*.

He recommended only a few, selected television programs to the students at the Maximo College and gave them tickets to the opera. "Because," he said, "you must know these things; it is important to know these things; this is culture; classical music and classical literature, this is culture."

Finally, he does listen to the radio, but only for classical music which at times he has on in the background when he is working or, according to the journalist Evangelina Himitian, sometimes to go to sleep.

57

R IS FOR...RECIPE FOR MIRACLES

If the Santa Fe daily, *El Litoral,* produced the headline that has passed into history, "Fr. Bergoglio's Miracles" (see "M is for...Miracles," p. 88), let's ask ourselves: What is the recipe for a miracle? And let us put on the table straightaway the two crucial ingredients: faith and self-denial. Or, faith and sacrifice. Or again, faith and love for the things that we do. But we can be certain that a recipe exists and Bergoglio provides it.

He did this when he was commenting upon the Gospel passage that recounts the miracle of miracles, the multiplication of the loaves and of the fish: "The disciples, at a loss in the face of the inadequacy of the means at their disposal, trusting in the words of Jesus, relieve the hunger of the crowd."

This teaches us that, in the Church as also in the world, a word we need not fear is *solidarity*—that is to say, knowing how to put at God's disposition what we have, namely, our humble capacities. That is because only by sharing, by giving, will our life bear fruit and be fruitful. Solidarity is a word not well regarded by the spirit of the world. Solidarity is the recipe for Bergoglio's miracles.

58.

R IS FOR...REFORMS

Only time will tell what will take place in this present pontificate. But there is one element, largely overlooked, which indicates clearly the mandate, if we can use this word, that the cardinals gave to Bergoglio—not in a personal sense (such a thing is not permitted)—but in general to the future pope. There is one element, which enables us to enter into the general congregations that preceded the conclave, and which makes it possible for us to understand what it was that the cardinals spoke about. It is Bergoglio himself who has revealed this element.

But let us proceed in an orderly fashion. On March 16, 2013, three days after the election, in his audience with journalists, Bergoglio explained why he took the name Francis (and we have seen this under "F is for...Francis," p. 51). He cited the amusing suggestions of his brothers, the cardinals.

> After that some people started making a few jokes: "You should take the name Adrian, because Adrian VI was a reformer and we need reform..." Another said to me, "No, No! You should take the name Clement XV. In that way

you could get your own back on Clement XIV, who suppressed the Society of Jesus." These were jokes.

If, after the election, while they were still in the Sistine Chapel, the theme of reforms was the object of often quite elaborate jokes between the cardinals and the newly elected pope, this must mean something.

59.

R IS FOR...ROSARY

"Fr. Bergoglio has a great devotion to Our Lady and prays the rosary always, always," I am told by those who know him well, repeating and reinforcing the point: "Always, always."

One day he was taking part in a meeting with the priests of the diocese. The work had been divided into two sessions, morning and afternoon, but the morning session had gone on longer than planned and the heat had done the rest. To sum it up, some of the points on the program they were discussing were well and truly skipped. In any case, after lunch, without any need to say so, they were all agreed on taking a break and on having a little rest.

In the meantime, those who had been invited to the afternoon session began to arrive. For a short time they gathered downstairs, then, when they began to be a significant number, they began climbing the stairs. They were expecting to find the bishops already at work. Instead, to their great surprise, the hall was completely empty. On the seats there was paper and the notes of those who were absent, but despite the timetable, there was still almost no one there.

Along the side wall, down at the end, walking with his head down, close to the windows, was Fr. Bergoglio. With a rosary in his hand, he was praying. While all the bishops were resting, the future pope was praying. He alone.

60.
S IS FOR...ST. JOSEPH

Alongside his great Marian devotion, Bergoglio has also developed a devotion to St. Joseph. When his vocation was unleashed while he was in confession on September 21, 1953, it was in a parish dedicated to San José de Flores—St. Joseph (of the area) of Flores. We do not know whether Bergoglio understood the significance of this at that moment. Nor can we say whether he noticed that the statue close to the confessional, which almost hears the words of the future pope, is that of St. Joseph. Then, as it turned out, the first parish entrusted to his care was dedicated to St. Joseph. It is behind the Maximo College of St. Joseph, of which he became rector.

Another connection to this great saint: Although the pope's election took place on March 13, 2013, the Mass for the inauguration of the pontificate took place six days later, on Tuesday, March 19 (the Feast of St. Joseph). The whole of the homily turned on the character of St. Joseph as guardian.

On Pope Francis's coat of arms, apart from the symbol of the Jesuits and the star representing Mary, there is the flower of nard, one of the emblems of St. Joseph. Finally, on June 19, 2013, after almost one hundred days of his pontificate, there was an evolution in Eucharistic prayers II, III, and IV of the Roman Missal. By will of the pope, after the name of Mary, it has become compulsory "to make mention of St. Joseph, her spouse," as was already the case in Eucharistic Prayer I. Thus, for example, Eucharistic Prayer II has become: "Have mercy on us all, we pray; that with the Blessed Virgin Mary, Mother of God, with St. Joseph, her spouse, with the blessed Apostles..."

61.

S IS FOR...SAINTS (MOST BELOVED)

One of the most loved saints in Argentina is St. Cajetan, patron saint of bread and of work. About the increasing devotion to this saint over the last fifteen years, Bergoglio has much to say to us.

In 1997, sixty-four days after Bergoglio's appointment as coadjutor archbishop of Buenos Aires, he took part in the procession in honor of St. Cajetan. This feast, held each year on August 7, is a solemn one.

As the journalist Evangelina Himitian recounts it, on that day six hundred thousand people stood in procession behind the Jesuit bishop. The people wanted to pray to St. Cajetan for bread and for work. Yet, it also became a sign to the government to stop manipulating its figures, and to deal with the crisis that was hurting every family in Argentina.

Before the shrine to the saint, at Liniers, two lines were formed. On the right were those who want to kiss the relics. On the left, those who want some objects to be blessed. There Bergoglio preached his first homily as coadjutor archbishop. "Work is sacred. If God has given us the gift of bread and of life, no one can take from us the gift of gaining that bread. Work, like bread, must be divided between all."

From that time onward, every year, the Feast of St. Cajetan has become an occasion for proclaiming anew justice in the name of God. The government has never been pleased with this.

62.

S IS FOR...SCHOOL

How did the future pope get on at school? Those who have been able to take a peek at the registers of the Coronel Pedro Cerviño Institute on the calle Varela (Varela Road), the school he attended as a child, say the mark for when he was six years old was "satisfactory."

Was he a good boy at school? Yes, but he was not overly studious. What subjects did he like? Literature, psychology, and religion. When he chose the professional technical institute, where he studied a great deal of chemistry, his friends were surprised. He was generous and was ready to help those who were smaller than he was. They recall him as a leader, but he did not impose himself. He was a person who stood out, someone you would notice, someone you could turn to if you had a problem and you could be sure that he would give you a hand.

63.

S IS FOR...SECRETARY

Fr. Martin was the secretary to Cardinal Antonio Quarracino, archbishop of Buenos Aires prior to Bergoglio. Cardinal Quarracino was a native of Pollica in the province of Salerno. He had left Pollica with his parents when he was four years old.

When Bergoglio became the new archbishop of the city in 1998, upon entering the diocesan offices he noticed Fr. Martin sitting at his desk. It was not the first time he had seen him, but this time he could not restrain himself and said: "Martin, you are a priest. What are you doing here? You need to go out among the people."

And so Fr. Martin returned to being a priest of the streets. For a limited time he helped the archbishop a little in the mornings but never in the afternoons. And so, if anyone went to see the archbishop after 3:00 P.M. they found him sitting at his desk and, if, while they were talking, the telephone rang, he would say, "Excuse me," and would answer the phone with, "Hello, Bergoglio here. Who is speaking?"

Bergoglio never wanted a secretary and, very rare among the cardinals, he arrived in Rome for the conclave alone. After the election, he did not have an assistant, so much so that it was Benedict XVI who gave him his.

Going back to the time at the diocesan offices in Buenos Aires, we meet Felix. Everyone knows him. He used to do the cleaning for the entrance to the diocesan offices. One day he was seen dressed up smartly with a tie and seated at a desk. "Monsignor Bergoglio has asked me to help him this morning," said Felix. That day, the janitor was the secretary. At other times it was an elderly woman who had made herself available. These, then, were the Buenos Aires assistants in the office to the future pope.

64.

S IS FOR...SICKNESS

The upper part of the pope's right lung is missing. It was removed in 1957, when he was twenty-one years old, after a time of terrible pain. Fr. Bergoglio recounted to Francesca Ambrogetti that for three days he lay between life and death. One day, overwhelmed by spasms, with a high temperature and exhausted, he clung to his mother like a small child and cried, "Tell me, what is happening to me!"

The doctors found three cysts on his lung, the cause of a serious attack of pneumonia. But before the cure arrived, with the operation and the removal, the Lord sent him powerful medicine. The religious sister arrived. She had known him from when he was a child, had prepared him for his First Holy Communion. She said to him, "You are following the example of Jesus."

It was the doctors who healed his body. But in his soul, it was Sister Dolores who, with those words, opened up to him, let us say, a perspective from "high above" that until then he had not had. To see the pope today, walking at a smart pace, sometimes limping a little, it seems strange to think that he has suffered a severe lung problem. Those who are close to him, though, know that after such exertions he needs to rest. But he tries not to make too much of it.

65.

S IS FOR...SIN

Hearing Bergoglio talk about sin is amazing. "For me, feeling you are a sinner is one of the best things that can happen to a person," he says in a book interview. The reason is that the sense of guilt, the shame, the awareness of error, can become a powerful fuel that can bring you directly to the confessional.

The confessional is not a simple "laundry" or "the dry-cleaner's." Neither is it a "seat of torture"—it is the place of encounter with God. To feel oneself a sinner, therefore, is a good thing, beautiful; or better, "the most beautiful thing that could happen" because it puts us in motion toward God, who is always waiting there to forgive us. There are alternatives to this motion and they are very serious.

On the one hand, there is the feeling that we are all right, self-sufficient, and without the need for God. On the other hand, there is that feeling of desperation, thinking that the sin is unforgiveable. But there is no sin that cannot be forgiven because there is no sin that is greater than the greatness of God.

If there is one concept that Bergoglio is always repeating, so that people may understand it, it is the greatness of God, the greatness of his mercy. Mercy and sin are the topics Pope Francis brings to our attention most frequently.

66.
S IS FOR...SUICIDE

It is instructive to read what Bergoglio thinks of suicide, of a person who commits it, a person who decides to put an end to it all. The Argentine pope once observed to Rabbi Skorka: "At one time those who had committed suicide were denied a funeral, and we know the reason why; one who commits suicide puts an end to the natural course of his or her own life by their own decision, something which only God can decide. But, pay attention: *Once upon a time!*"

And then the pope added, "I maintain respect for such a person, because such a person has not succeeded in overcoming the adversities of their existence. I do not turn away such a person. I entrust him or her to the mercy of God."

67.

T IS FOR... TANGO

Francesca Ambrogetti once asked Fr. Bergoglio whether he likes the tango. "Oh, yes," the pope replied. "Very much."

He likes to dance the tango, and he did so for a long time as a young man. He knows some pieces by heart and quotes them and, obviously, knows how to interpret them. His preferences, though, are for the orchestra of D'Arienzo, for Carlos Gardel, but also for Astor Piazzolla. He knew Azucena Maizani personally and also administered extreme unction to him.

68.

T IS FOR...TELEPHONE CALLS

Adriano only put out the lamp thirty seconds ago, or so it seems. In reality, four hours have shot by. He went to bed at 4:30 A.M. and it's not yet even 9:00 A.M. And there is his father knocking at the door of his room.

One day, coming back from work, Adriano had called into the curia and had left a card there. It had on it his name, address, and telephone number and with it was a request to be able to speak to Fr. Bergoglio, who was now cardinal. Adriano had been a drug addict. He had abandoned drugs in a way that his friends did not understand. Some of them even laughed about it. He had stopped being a drug addict through prayer. According to him, it was the prayers of his mother, Paola, that had saved him. She had a great devotion to Our Lady of Luján. He was healed.

And now his father was knocking at the door. He hasn't even had five hours sleep!

"Dad, what's the matter? I was late last night and now I want to sleep a bit," Adriano says.

"You are wanted on the telephone."

"Not now, please. I will call back later."

"Adriano. It is Fr. Bergoglio." Adriano leapt out of bed and picked up the phone.

"I am Fr. Bergoglio. Hello, Adriano. I know that you wanted to speak to me. Did I wake you up?"

The next day Adriano is face-to-face with Cardinal Bergoglio.

69.

T IS FOR...TERESINA (THÉRÈSE OF LISIEUX)

Teresina is St. Thérèse of Lisieux, the young French mystic, Carmelite nun, and Doctor of the Church who passed from this life when she was only twenty-four years old. In her diary she wrote, "I will spend my Heaven doing good on Earth. I will send down a shower of roses."

On the basis of these words, in 1925, a Jesuit, Fr. Putigan, composed a novena to her (praising the Holy Trinity), asking her to do him a favor and to give him a sign. In this case, the request was granted. As a sign he asked, in fact, for a rose. To his great surprise, after three days, the rose arrived, as did the grace he had requested.

He repeated the novena, asking for a further grace and a rose, and once again he received both the rose and the favor. In this way the "Novena of the Roses" (also known as the "Novena of the Twenty-Four Glory Bes") began to spread, and be considered a holy and a powerful novena through which Thérèse intercedes and brings reassurance.

In Cardinal Bergoglio's room in Buenos Aires you could see a photograph of St. Thérèse and always many white roses to adorn it. Bergoglio admits to always having had a great devotion to her, to praying to her always and to having received, like Fr. Putigan, confirmation of the request by the gift of a rose.

70.

T IS FOR...THIRTEEN

In Bergoglio's life the number thirteen recurs in a way that is both odd and significant. At thirteen months he began staying with his grandmother, Rosa, a presence of fundamental importance to his personal development and his spiritual growth.

On December 13, 1969, he was ordained as a priest by Archbishop Ramón José Castellano.

On May 13, 1992, the Apostolic Nuncio, Monsignor Ubaldo Calabresi, informed him, seven days ahead of the official communication, that he had been appointed auxiliary bishop of Buenos Aires.

On March 13, 2013—the thirteenth day of the thirteenth year—Bergoglio was elected pope on that unforgettable evening of the "Brothers and sisters, good evening."

And it is to chapter 13, verse 13, of the Gospel of St. John that Bergoglio always seems to entrust his priestly ministry:

> You call me Master and Lord, and rightly so because so I am. If I then, the Lord and Master, have washed your feet, you too must wash one another's feet. I have given you an example, so that you may do likewise. (John 13:13–15)

71.

T IS FOR...THREATS

Did Fr. Bergoglio ever receive any threats? I have asked this question of many people who know Pope Francis at close hand, but no one knows anything. If the answer is yes, then it is likely that he never said a word about it to anyone, so as not to frighten them, perhaps so as not to have to accept limitations upon his pastoral work, trusting only in Providence. We know that he frequented the Villas Miserias, the dwellings of the shantytowns, and that this could have annoyed some people. We know that he defended people disliked by Videla's regime, hiding them and helping them to flee. And we know that he was always in the midst of the people, easily accessible. And so?

It is certain that his more exposed priests received threats. Among them was Fr. José Maria Di Paola, called Fr. Pepe, a young man of Italian (Calabrian) origin, with a small beard. As Bergoglio recounted to Gianni Valente, one evening in April 2009, a well-dressed man, with an accent from the capital, and therefore not from the Villa Miserias, halts Fr. Pepe who is returning home on his bicycle.

"Are you Fr. Pepe?" asks the well-dressed man. "If you don't stop, we'll take you out. We have sworn it."

What wrong had the priest done? What did he have to "stop"? He had complained that in the Villas they were selling drugs openly. A free market, as remunerative as it was shameful.

Fr. Pepe mentions this to Bergoglio, who begins to pray. He goes down on his knees, before the Blessed Sacrament, with a request. "What should he do? What is to be done, now that our priests are risking their lives for you? What am I to do for them?"

During his prayer, he finds a path that he will follow with courage and with immediate effect. He decides to make this threat public, without revealing the identity of the priest. He does this at the end of a homily. It was enough. They never so much as touched Fr. Pepe, just as they never did anything to the open-house centers of welcome or the structures opened by the diocese in the Villas Miserias.

72.

U IS FOR...UNCLES

Or rather, great-uncles, his grandfather's brothers, who had emigrated to Argentina in 1922. Fr. Bergoglio quotes them as an example of the courage his family is capable of.

His great-uncles worked very hard in Argentina. They succeeded in building themselves a block of four stories. It is in Paraná and one of the first buildings with a lift in the whole of the city. With family and Italian pride it is called "Palazzo Bergoglio"—the Bergoglio Building.

Then came the Great Crisis, and in 1932 they had to sell everything and start again from scratch. Jorge's grandfather also had to ask for a loan to start afresh, while his father lost his job, but, Bergoglio recalls, he did not lose his spirit.

Jorge, a child of another generation and of a different period, certainly one that was less dramatic, is very impressed by the capacity of his own forefathers in overcoming the difficulties of life: "It is a demonstration of the power of their spirit," he says as photographs and the names connected to them from his childhood pass before his eyes.

Overcoming difficulties is something people today are asking of Pope Francis.

73.
V is for…Villas Miserias (Misery Villages)

Speaking of journeys, there are not only the journeys to and from Rome. The journey closest to Bergoglio's heart is the daily journey he made on the number 70 bus to the Villas Miserias, the shantytown of Buenos Aires with its mud huts, where forty-five thousand people live on the streets, streets with no tarmac, earthen streets that turn to mud when it rains.

The people live in the midst of rats and of electric wires that run chaotically above their heads casting a sense of looming tragedy. There is dirt and there is chaos and the inhabitants do not even have the comfort of having a prestigious name or the name of a saint who assumes responsibility for their street, because there the streets have no names, only numbers, which go from twenty-one to twenty-four.

Bergoglio used to go there, dressed as a priest, even when he was a cardinal. He used to go into their houses, speak to the people, joke with the children. He became the friend of everyone. He is the one who battled so that the children should always be baptized, irrespective of the matrimonial situation of their parents, regular or otherwise. The many processions in honor of the saints were his idea. Likewise the celebrations for the church dedicated to the Virgin of Caacupé. He was the source of security for those priests who were most exposed and who were most often threatened. He was the shield of the poor. They returned the kindness by affectionate requests for photographs together. Even today Bergoglio is the most photographed person on the walls of the huts of the poor of Buenos Aires.

74.

V IS FOR...VOCATION

On September 21, 1953, Bergoglio's life changed completely. That he recalls in detail dates, persons, and situations after so many years is extra proof of this. That day, a student feast day, he was going to meet his friends at the station. Suddenly, he found himself in front of St. Joseph's church. He decided to go in to make his confession. He did not know the priest there, had never met him before, but something happened that was unique, great, and supernatural.

In his own words: "Something strange happened to me during that confession and I don't know exactly what it was, but it changed my life. I would say I let myself be surprised when my guard was down. I became aware that he was waiting for me. From that moment onward for me God is he who 'goes ahead of you.'"

In the course of that confession, Jorge clearly felt himself to be called by God, who "was waiting for him." It is very rare to encounter vocations that are born so unexpectedly.

These are not decisions that are made by pressing a button. They are the fruit of a natural process of maturation, at times even of a struggle within oneself and with God. For Bergoglio, no. And the first person to be surprised by this was himself.

So, his choice to become a priest began with an intimate call: a spectacular, hidden, but all-encompassing and really overwhelming call. Young Jorge emerged from the church so completely overcome that he returned home at once. He gave up his evening with his friends (including his girlfriend). He would not talk about his life-changing experience with anyone for four years.

In the meantime, he finished high school and continued his work. But God had revealed himself. And Jorge had understood. And, even if the matter had remained between him and God, his dad and his grandmother had detected something. At the age of twenty-one, he entered the diocesan seminary and then, almost immediately, chose the Jesuits with the dream, which he was never able to realize, of becoming a missionary to Japan. But other journeys and other missions awaited him.

75.

W is for...When (They Come to Confession)

Alfonso knelt down in the confessional. He greeted the priest, but he did not recognize him. He began his confession.

Bergoglio listens, and at the end he asks him, "Do you give to the poor?"

Alfonso answers, "Yes."

Bergoglio continues, "And do you touch the hand of the poor person?"

Alfonso does not understand.

The priest persisted. "When you give money to the poor, do you touch the hand of the poor person or do you let the money drop from a height?"

"No. It is not really right to say that I drop the money from a height"—Alfonso is embarrassed—"but...well, no, I don't touch their hand. I avoid doing so."

"And do you look them in the face?"

"No," says Alfonso.

Fr. Bergoglio stays quiet. He has no more to say, and Alfonso understands. There was no evil intended on Alphonso's part, only a certain lack of care. All of a sudden the superficiality of his attitude presents itself as a matter to be concerned about, to be sorry for.

76.

W IS FOR...WHEN (I DO NOT GIVE COMMUNION)

Why is it, they used to ask in Buenos Aires, that at times Cardinal Bergoglio does not distribute Communion? Not always, but sometimes in Buenos Aires, yes, it does happen.

At Mass there are important people taking part, highly placed individuals, well-off, famous, whose reputations may provoke some gossip. In any case they are people who, if asked, would be generous and munificent. They are sitting in the front row and are excited to be there with the cardinal, with the photographer ready to take photographs to be put on the Internet and sent to the newspapers.... On such occasions Bergoglio, to the disappointment of those in the front rows, distributes Communion only to the altar servers and to the deacons.

Does this happen only by chance? Is he tired? No. It is a very precise choice. He explains why in his dialogue with Rabbi Skorka.

> Among the parishioners, there are those who have killed, not only intellectually or physically, but indirectly, by paying unjust wages. It may be that they form part of charitable organizations, but

they do not pay their workers or they pay them unofficially in cash. It is hypocrisy. It is schizophrenia. For this reason on some occasions, I do not distribute Communion because I do not want them to approach me for the photos.

This is an understandably hard attitude, reserved for those who not only are not repentant but who live in a state of declared ambiguity between an evil which they practice and a good that is only opportunistic. Something that Bergoglio cannot stand.

77.

W is for…When
(There Is a Price List in the Parish)

He takes her hand and helps her go down the steps of the entrance. Inside it is dark, but it is very fresh. They look around in search of the parish priest, but he is not there. However, there is a door that is open and on it a sign, written by hand, "Parish Office." They approach it and say timidly, "We have to…we want to get married."

A woman keeps her head down without looking at their faces. She asks, "Have you chosen the date?"

"Yes. We were thinking of the twelfth of July this year."

"Let's see. The twelfth of July, twelfth of July…is free. Good. This is the list, as you can see …"

"Excuse me. What list?"

"The price list. As you can see, on Sundays, there is a supplement. This here is the base price."

"Excuse us once more. This list is for what?"

"Do you want to get married or not? These are the prices for getting married in this church. Work day or rest day; evening or morning. With or without a red carpet. There's a price for everything."

Juan and Manila look at each other quizzically. They are more offended by the tone than by the prices. In any case, they choose the basic package. Deposit. Receipt. Thank you and good-bye.

There are many couples like Juan and Manila, and Bergoglio will not accept it. "This is making a market out of worship." The idea the cardinal used to try to communicate to his priests and to the people is that you cannot buy anything with money in the Church. You can only make a contribution, freely, on the basis of what you can afford. Remember the widow in the Gospel who appears to give very little. However, as Jesus explains, in reality she has given a great deal (as we read in Mark 12:41–44). The offering in church, in the end, is a sharing in something, not a setting out of wares as in a shop.

78.
W IS FOR...WOMEN

One day, when speaking about his grandmother, Rosa, Pope Francis said, "I received the first proclamation of Christianity from this woman, from my grandmother. That is very beautiful; the first proclamation, at home, in my family."

Every word he said about his grandmother produced a smile, and in his eyes I could sense an evocation of this extraordinary woman, to whom Bergoglio owes everything. Yes, as he says, he received the first proclamation of Christianity in the family. He received this by voice and by witness from a very specific person, from a woman, from his grandmother. This is not an accident.

"This makes me think," he says, "of the love of so many mothers and of so many grandmothers in the transmission of the faith. They are the ones who transmit the faith. This is what happened also in the earliest times because St. Paul said to Timothy, "I remember the faith of your mother and of your grandmother." All you mothers and grandmothers, who are here, remember this! Transmit the faith."

Once he was asked what a society would be like that was just male. "Austere, harsh, and deprived of sacredness," he said—not a response that would endear him to men.

And then what about women? We could synthesize his thinking like this: they bring tenderness and maternity to the world. Women welcome society, contain it, and transform it into community. If there were another word for women, it could be "gift." It is true that only a man can become a priest, like Jesus. However, citing a monk from the second century, the great realities of Christianity are all feminine: the Church, the soul, and, of course, Mary. Meanwhile, among his collaborators in the curia, there are many laypeople and not a few women.

79.

W IS FOR... WORK

The summer of his third year in middle school brought something really new to young Jorge. In a way it was quite surprising to him, but in reality not so surprising for a family of the 1950s emigrants with a high regard for work. His father, Mario, told him of his decision: "I thought that this year, during the holidays, you could begin to work. I will try to find something for you."

Jorge was not expecting this and was amazed. At the end of the day, there was nothing lacking in their home. And, in fact, his father's purpose was not to balance the family budget but to get the young man used to work.

A short time after this Jorge begins. For two years he will be doing the cleaning in a shoe factory before moving on to the administrative department. Later on, he is taken on by the analytical laboratory of Hickethier and Bachmann, where he works in the mornings, while in the afternoons, he attends the industrial institute, specializing in food chemistry.

When thinking back to those years, Bergoglio feels a profound sense of gratitude toward those who persuaded him to work and toward those he met when he was working. Pope Francis, who has worked, knows what work is like and what difficulties and joys women and men encounter every day.

80

Y IS FOR...YOUNG PEOPLE

For thousands of young people in St. Joseph Parish, Fr. Bergoglio, their parish priest, was the inventor of the cinema. Yes, because in the entire neighborhood in the 1980s, there wasn't a single place for films to be screened. Children were growing up without ever having seen a film, without having experienced cinema. Bergoglio felt very badly about these young people who were denied everything.

However, the Jesuit Maximo College, in the parish, had a large, comfortable hall for cinema screenings, and so the order was clear: Let's open that hall up to the neighborhood.

Every Sunday, at a different time from the catechism, a film was projected. It was a great burden for the young men of the Maximo College who had to do the cleaning before and after. But it was a task they undertook happily.

"Make the young people happy; make them laugh, let them enjoy themselves," Fr. Bergoglio used to say to the future Jesuit priests who conducted these gatherings. He did not say, "Evangelize them," but, "Make them happy."

Those children of that time are now around forty years old, and almost all of them have children of their own. Their children are all baptized and are the pride of "grandfather" Bergoglio.

Epilogue

Having come to the end of this book, there are several conclusions open to us. We can simply put it to one side as an interesting thing to have read. We can perhaps marvel at the goodness of the man about whose life and thoughts we have learned so much. We might find ourselves grateful that a bishop of the Church should have such ability to be so close to people, particularly those most vulnerable or in need. There may well be something of a reaction that he belongs to a rather different world than the one we experience, and we may even have criticisms as to some of his decisions and pronouncements. I would like to suggest, however, that this book presents us with a challenge. This is not just a book of quotations that, having been read, should be put on the shelf. The real value lies in the questions that it asks of us.

In these pages we see the roots of Pope Francis's living spirituality. In a very honest way he has opened himself to us and told us not only about himself but how he sees the Church and its place in the world in which we live today. He has shown us how each one of us can use the message of the Gospel to direct our decisions and our actions. And he has shown us how much there is to be done. There can be no complacency about the world in which we live. A billion people on this planet go to bed each night hungry, lacking even minimal nourishment. While we have the drugs to cure all manner of disease and illness, millions die simply because the drugs are not made available to them. Over a billion people do not have access to the most basic commodity for life—clean water. Millions of others suffer under forms of political oppression and are denied basic human rights. All too many live in constant fear of the violent incursions of militias and paramilitary groups. There are others who are the victims of multinational companies and the greed that is generated by modern economic systems.

There is the mistrust and violence born of religious persecution, often where religion is used as a political agenda. Millions live as refugees, driven from their homeland. Nor must we forget the victims of the unseen and unpredicted environmental disasters, such as earthquakes, hurricanes, and typhoons, and those who are becoming the victims of climate change. Yes, there is so much to be done. Pope Francis firmly points out that we can all be part of the solution and that we cannot abdicate our responsibility and must not leave solutions to the decisions of governments, or "some other."

I think that probably the greatest achievement of what Pope Francis is saying to us in these pages is that he is making us all feel uncomfortable and challenged about how seriously we allow our faith to challenge who we are and to influence our daily lives.

In his Apostolic Exhortation Evangelii Gaudium (The Joy of the Gospel), Pope Francis tells us about his vision for the new evangelization and the call to each and every one of us, without exception, to be "missionary disciples." That is what we are called to be, by virtue of our baptism. In the increasingly secular and cosmopolitan world in which we live, there is more urgency than ever that we should live our faith in our actions and have our faith guiding our decisions.

The Gospel speaks to every circumstance, and it calls us to stand against what is wrong. Sometimes we can identify immediately what is wrong. On other occasions it may take wisdom and further reflection and discernment to recognize the mistakes that we make and to admit that we have made the wrong decisions or have misunderstood the problem and endorsed the wrong "solution."

Pope Francis is asking us, as Christians and as Catholics—and all people who seek what is good and true—to recognize the possibilities that we have to make our world a better place. For all too many of us, religious practice has been too readily identified with "keeping the rules." That observance of rules and regulations can give us a comfortable feeling of belonging and identifying with a particular group. It can also allow us the mistaken feeling that we are doing enough. The Gospel has little to say about rules. In fact, it is in the Gospels that we so often see Jesus being so critical of those, like the Pharisees and the Sadducees, who seemed to judge themselves as "righteous" if they kept the rules. Jesus is quick to point out that they have, in fact, missed the point. They have failed to see the meaning of the most important commandments. Those commandments are about the love of God and loving your neighbor as yourself. Jesus called us to extend our horizons to the good that we can do, the compassion that we can bring, the suffering that we can alleviate when we allow our lives to be motivated by love. Love calls us to stretch the boundaries of possibility. This is the Gospel message that Francis is determined to place before us again, as our collective and our personal challenge.

If you return to the pages of this book, there are numerous occasions when the text is not just speaking about the thoughts and actions of Pope Francis or of Archbishop Jorge Bergoglio. The text is speaking to us and asking us to question our motives and our aspirations.

In these pages we have the portrait of a man who sees nothing exceptional in himself. He claims frequently, even as pope, that he makes mistakes and gets things wrong. He is just like the rest of us. But when we recognize our own failings, we cannot say that we are therefore not good enough and have no role in making our world a better place. We must acknowledge our mistakes, the things that we get wrong, and learn from them.

In his first year as pope, Francis has challenged just about everyone. In the Consistory of February 2014 he created eighteen new cardinals, and he told them, in no uncertain terms, that this was not a promotion but a calling into deeper and more humble service of the Church. He asked them to work together, bringing their experience of so many different and diverse parts of the Church to their role in advising and assisting the pope.

He has challenged bishops, telling them that they must not compromise on their ministry for fear of making mistakes. They must not sit in their churches, merely inviting people to come in. They must have the courage to go out and to walk with people, even when they are walking away from the Church. He told the Ambassadors of the Holy See to serve in humility and not to cultivate any sense of self-importance. He has spoken about the qualities that are required of those called to be bishops. They must, above all else, be pastors who do not forget the smell of their sheep! He has been clear about the qualities of those studying for the priesthood. They must be growing in compassion, pastoral care, and good preaching lived out in the example of their lives. He has spoken to members of religious orders about the generosity of the vowed life.

The Apostolic Exhortation *Evangelii Gaudium* (The Joy of the Gospel) challenges all of us, without exception. He speaks of the role of women in the Church, the value of family life, the place of parishes and their communities, and he tells us all that we are "missionary disciples." So you and I are called to reflect on ourselves—our gifts, our talents, our abilities. What have we been given by God so that we can be missionary disciples? We must discover our gifts and use them. Look back at those pages in which we have learned so much about this new Pope Francis. How can our knowledge of him help us in our own vocation?

The Most Reverend John Arnold
Bishop of the Diocese of Salford
Province of Liverpool, England

Acknowledgments

Thanks to Fr. José Gabriel Funes, SJ, director of the Vatican Speculum, to Fr. Guillermo Ortiz, SJ, chief editor of Radio Vatican's Spanish channel for Europe and for Latin America, to Nelson Pollicelli, and to all those who have dedicated their time to me, to enable me to know better the Argentina of the last forty years. There are many ways of receiving people. The way you received me was one of authentic Christian witness.

I would like also to thank Francesca Ambrogetti and Sergio Rubin, to whom I would say that, through their interview with Cardinal Bergoglio of 2010, they have offered to the whole world a very sensitive kind of visiting card of the new pope.

ABOUT THE AUTHOR

Rosario Carello (b. 1973), journalist, is the author and
presenter of Rai Uno's *A Sua Immagine* (*In His Image*),
and he works with Famiglia Cristiana (The Christian
Family). On Good Friday 2011, he interviewed Pope
Benedict XVI. He has worked for TV 2000. He began
working in radio when he was seventeen years old, and
he collaborates with various papers and with *Carello
Editore*. He directs the blog www.rosariocarello.it.